Autobiography of
and
Ponderings on
A Boy and his Journey

Via therapeutic writings

by
jimmie joe

ISBN: 0-7596-5966-4

This book is printed on acid free paper.

1stBooks - rev. 2/28/02

In fond remembrance;

Norma Jean Zentmyer
Helen L. Ritter
June Weaver

World Trade Center
1 November, 2001

This book (A Boy and his Journey) was written long before the tragic event of the 09/11/01 terrorist attack on the Twin Towers and our Pentagon.

Now, for the first time since World War Two, we are engaged in a war in which America's people are united, it is without question, a "Just Cause".

We can not allow this type of terrorism to thrive in a world shrunk to a timeline less then 20 hours by air from anywhere on earth, a world where terrorists are, for all practicable purposes, right next door.

Now that we are united in a war for the very survival of our of Freedoms, our Children's Freedom's, it will be interesting as to the American people's resolve in what will be a prolonged and casualty filled engagement, at home and abroad. Pray God we hang in there until this scourge on mankind is eliminated, cell-by-cell and in every sponsoring country.

We have come a long way in destroying the foe while keeping the innocent civilian losses at a minimum. (Civilians killed in World War Two averaged 385,000 a _month!!_) We have dropped over 3,000 bombs on Afghanistan in about three weeks, less then two-dozen have caused casualties thru human error or malfunction, this is an amazing record and a tribute to our caring about innocent lives.

My pain and anger at the huge losses of innocents in our earlier wars show in my writings, some losses will occur but _I really believe we now try to keep the killing of civilians from taking place._ ("Collateral damage" is a word I don't like; it's too damn sterile).

My prayers go with mankind for all races and religions and may God Bless America
  jimmie joe

Memorial Day, 2001,

24th. Inf. Div., 34th. /21st., Inf. Reg. — 1950/51

I thank my fallen Comrades and it matters not if they fell at Valley Forge, the North or South in our Civil War, nor any War, be it as large as World War II or as small as peacekeeping in the Balkans. It matters not if they fell in a War some of our Countrymen believe was wrong, or a War "I" believe not just and it matters not if they fell in a training accident.

It matters not if a Cross, a Star of David, a Crescent Moon, or any other inscription carved in stone identifies their mound of earth, and it matters not the Race of the one who rests below.

These have nothing to do with the honour I bestow on our men and women who die in harms way, and they have nothing to do with how I feel on a Day such as this. Memorial Day brings back sadness with a bit of pain, reminding me there is infinitely more pain carried for a lifetime by the Moms, Dads, Wives, Children and all who love their Warrior dead.

One-day a year set aside for remembrance is minuscule, enjoy your long weekend but please take a moment for a prayer of thanks.

> I honour you my Warrior Brothers,
> I'll join you in a while.
> Will you welcome me as Comrade brave?
> or will there be no smile?
>
> Have I upheld your sacrifice and death
> as I lived time you never had?
> Is our Homeland as Free as when you left?
> By "Gods own truth" your answer is —————?
> Your answer friend ————— is mine.

Although our Warriors were young men, in my olden mind we were Boys, with much honour and respect I shall refer to them as such.

jimmie joe
fishhook junction, alaska

Précis

1997 — My writing began in long hand aboard my cabin cruiser, "Old White Guy", while anchored at Peaceful Halibut Cove, Alaska.

why?.....

Seven years ago I tried to talk,
it did not do any good.
My children grown did kind of balk,
they never understood.

That was all right, I should have known,
no way they could understand.
Even tho my kids were fully grown,
I never tried to talk again.

Fall, 1989

In the early fall of nineteen eighty-nine everything came apart for me, I nearly was not here to be writing what has turned out to be these books. I now know I'm not unique, but at the time I was lost in the confusion of my inability to cope with a bit of time from a thirty-nine year old war and in the confusion of the lost I had become my nemesis.

About four months later, in January of Nineteen-ninety, I tried to talk with a few of my children, Denise, Tom and Cathie, adults in their thirties, of the tormented time my soul was going thru, it didn't work. In all honesty I don't see how it could have accomplished much as I had no specific concept at all about what I needed to reveal. I simply blubbered virtually incoherent about it being the war.

My ignorance of the WHY along with the confused distress of my mind probably left them scratching their heads and wondering a bit about their dad. I remained near the abyss from which my Angel had saved me four months earlier and was desperate for someone to help me. I didn't know who to ask, I didn't know how to ask and I didn't want to expose my perceived weakness with someone I didn't have a great deal of trust in.

I remained a bit lost for eight more years before, thru fury with the revelations in Eisenhower's Papers, the courage came. My writings, began in anger, became an outpouring I seemed unable to end, they ended with the healing of fluctuating distress carried for nearly fifty years.

I retired in 1984 and the last of my Children left home in 1985, my home increasingly became an empty, lonely place. Grandchildren's house filling laughter was replaced by echoing demons in the silence of night. These demons, I had kept leashed for nearly forty years, snapped their leash and had their moment. I was in mounting despair and adrift without a tangible clue something was deeply wrong and, as it turned out, I could no longer avoid the fates. My once peaceful cabin on the Little Susitna River nearly became my Armageddon, the Fishhook Bar became my refuge, and my writings, without question, became my emancipation.

Page 108, the drunk

> It'll take about four years or so,
> clock ticks slowly at the first.
> He'll begin frequenting the Fishhook Bar
> and the cause will not be thirst

After those many years to die due to a minds unresolved conflict seems irrational now, thru research I found it is not rare for Veterans of combat, the Ghosts of past battle zones are and remain imprinted rather well. I needed someone quite badly. No one was there. No one knew.

I don't know why I lost my ability to cope and became horribly lost, it's chilling when I think of what very nearly came to pass. There was not one cell of my brain that said, "hey boy come on, get help somewhere". What is disconcerting prior to the final crescendo of that hellish night is my mind held only one deadly answer, it was as if I had on blinders and there was only one direction, one path.

Page 109, Fall of nineteen eighty-nine,

> His forty-one mag he took to bed,
> silently told his friends good-bye.
> Cocked it and pressed it to his head
> about an inch behind right eye.

x

I told some Children of this in 1999, some will not know until they read this. No one would have known had I not written this book.

In the end visions of a Friend or Daughter finding my body overcame the fates and in darkness of my desolation I cried out for God. My Angel arrived and my Angel answered, giving me time. Even tho I was not aware of this gift for years, I am now tremendously thankful.

The next day my Daughter Cynthia and my Grand Children, Christopher and Jessica, stopped by to visit, Lord, what I nearly caused in their life's memory banks is something I don't like to contemplate.

I endured, even tho I would neither be aware of, nor consciously seek, my pressing need of healing for another eight years. The Boy who went to war remained behind the grief filled walls he had escaped to in1950. 48 years would pass before my courage came and I set Boy free. I am astonished and grateful for what Boys freedom has bestowed on me.

About January 1990

I think they thought their dad was weak,
grown daddies should be strong.
My crying when I tried to speak,
I felt they thought me wrong.
I never did get to the part
that pained my soul, that tore my heart.

I'd kept wounds masked nearly forty years
before disclosure made me cry.
It did not work with family.
Must there be pain 'til I die?

No, seven years has passed,
alone this time I'll try. Alone I'll cry.

Mid-Nov., 1997-Mar.,98

I did try, I tried alone, I cried alone, and I wrote this nomadic, healing book from a series of inter-related distressing and sorrowful trips back thru time alone. I forced a nineteen-year-old Soldier Boy cringing and kicking from the painful safety of "my hiding place" and into the light where I could see him. I'd fight him and he'd beg, I'd beg him and he'd cry. I got him drunk and that nineteen-year-old Soldier Boy completely kicked my ass and demanded relief from his anguished journey.

I'm to old for battle, a battle which had been untenable at the beginning, became skirmishes most of the years and raged as all out war at the end; I gave up the fight and, with what had to be Gods help, I won our freedom. I released Boys pain with tear filled writings and, with the tears I was able to say, "Welcome Home Son", it's alright now, it's over.

Page 112, I gave up, I fought no more

Damn it God won't you help me,
I don't want to die alone.
I am lost in pains direction.
The roads been long, please God, *please help*.

His demon fates had nearly taken him
to that land beyond the sky.
His Angel touched him just in time:
jimmie joe, **Hey!** *jimmie joe.*
Come on Boy it's time to cry.

All those years I thought Boy departed because he wanted to stay in "his safe place". I was wrong, Boy wanted out, I forced Boy to stay veiled; it was "my safe place ". I somehow created walls when I was the Boy and, as the Man, my misguided place of refuge became Boys prison.

Back then we knew naught about posttraumatic stress; there was no such name, *let alone the varying degrees of it.* We lived with it or we died from it, our life would seem normal to everyone except ourselves and overall mine was excluding the revelations this book is about. They were not debilitating but they were, at times, quite difficult to deal with. The conscious or subconscious gaining of knowledge by the long search for adjustment, and muddling through, were periods of my life not pleasant.

Unbidden visions from my war frequently popped-up inside my head, coping became a way of life. I made it through and survived as well as most. Why my crisis came so late in life is an enigma I doubt if I will ever unravel, possibly the last of my Children leaving home and my retirement within the same year left me vulnerable to an internal conflict I had carried for, at the time, about forty years.

Page 127, 1951 thru 1997,

I thought something was wrong with me,
a weakness I must hide.
The hurting, flitting pain I'd see,
I must hold back deep inside.

Page 71, October, 1950
Southern North Korea, two small Children

I do know they slept, if I hastened their death with too much morphine I just don't know. I had no idea back then I would carry those four pained and haunting eyes mirrored in my head for most of my life, my secret pain and hidden sorrow. I pray they didn't awaken except to Gods caring arms in heaven.

Page 112 —1998 a time to cry

Tears gushed from the old Warriors eyes
but they were not old Warriors tears,
the tears were from a Soldier Boy
who's age was nineteen years.

Page 72, Atonement?

Their eyes no longer dulled by pain,
a sparkle's what now shows.
They walk while holding hands with me,
we walk in summers sunshine
and we play in winters snows.

Of course it's all within my mind,
to my soul it is quite real.
My lines absolved near fifty years
we shared that dying field.

I am now at peace with time served in the Land of the Morning Calm. My dead rest where they belong and two small Korean Children's eyes have closed, and they, my Kim and my Leaha, rest a well-deserved rest, I've kept them up a very long time.

jimmie joe
fishhook junction, alaska

Index

Any single poem, with due credits, of this publication may be reproduced, transmitted, transcribed or translated into any language in any form without the written permission from the author, an amount more than one poem must have written permission.

Certain facts are gleaned from the Internets military history section.
<

HYPERLINKS:
"http://about.delphi.com/n/main.asp?=abusmilitary&nav=messages&msg=2092.1"

http://www.cfcsc.dnd.ca/links/milhist/korea.html

http://www.kimsoft.com/korea/kr-warv.htm

http://www.koreanwar-educator.org/Home.htm"

www.thehistorynet.com/MilitaryHistory/articles/2000/0400_text.html

http://www.geocities.com/Pentagon/1953/

http://www.thehistorynet.com/MilitaryHistory/articles/0496_cover.htm
>

"Korea the First Year" By;—James F. Schnabel"

Completed in the 50th Anniversary Year of the Korean War.

e-mail
alaska1960@yahoo.com

Dedicated with thankful appreciation

Malcolm Van Zant, my Father since I was three years old. Dad's impact on my person as I grew to adulthood was inspiring; I could not have asked more. I thank God Dad was in my life.
I thank you, I miss you, and I love you Dad.

My Alaska, a wondrous land I love.
Cy St Amond, my young friend of over twenty years.
R. Dean Foster, rest in peace fishing Buddy.
"Old Gent", my dog, he made my childhood a joy.

Members of the U.S. House risked their political careers as part of the House Management team in Clintons impeachment. With Clintons high popularity polls they showed courage where others failed miserably. I salute them with Honour.

Bob Barr, Ed Bryant, Steve Buyer, Charles Canady, Chris Cannon, Steve Chabot, George Gekas, Lindsey Graham, Asa Hutchinson, Bill McCollum, Henry Hyde, James Rogan, and James Sensenbrenner.

General Mark Clark, Fought for our abandoned POWs.
Helen Chenoweth-Hage, Protector of article Ten, Bill of Rights.
Larry Craig, Protector of article Ten, Bill of Rights.
Blanquita Cullum, a teacher of an individuals obligations.
Friends, at Fishhook Junction, Alaska, who I care for very much.
Ken Hamblin, a teacher of an individuals obligations.
Wayne archer "Johnnie" Johnson, Thank you Johnnie.
President John F. Kennedy, I just loved the guy.
Robert Kennedy, I had high hopes.
Rush Limbaugh, a teacher of an individuals obligations.
Pope John Paul II, a man of Peace, a man of God.
Michael Reagan, a teacher of an individuals obligations.
President Ronald Reagan, God bless you Ronnie.
General Mathew Ridgeway, a leader we needed.
Dr. Laura Schlessinger, a teacher of an individuals obligations.

xvii

Alan Simpson, protector of article Ten, Bill of Rights.
General James Van Fleet, fought for our abandoned POWs.
My surveyor Buddies, far to many to name, I think of you often.

A time distraught

Page — 70

Two small Children crumpled by the crossroads
with no one else around.
Two casualties of grown-ups war,
soon little bodies in the ground.

These two small Children were and are the *main* reason for my writings, they are why I sometimes rambled and repeated a bit as I typed and searched, typed and searched some more. I didn't know where or how to begin, God alone knows how many one-fingered pages I've typed and discarded. I wrote in circles around subjects the anguish of my mind knew was there but refused to release, all the while not knowing the direction I was going and not even quite sure why my journey had began.

It became matter of courage. Courage to face the Boys anguishes, courage to face the Children, *especially the Children,* courage to face my Comrades-in-arms and my Foe. The courage to express my deep sorrow, courage to admit they lived, courage to say I will remember and courage to feel I care they had died. I hid my grief of past reality, I fooled the world, I could not fool the anguish that lived inside where none could see, *I knew,* others at times may have suspected but they never knew WHY.

Page - 72

We had to leave them to die alone,
they died alone in sleep.
I knew no way could I atone,
for years my Soul would weep.

I'll never understand why this one piece of time so overwhelmed all my other unpleasant wartime trials and tribulations, and why I have taken so long, so very long, to heal.

Page, 106

It took 'til old age, all those years,
for me to get things right.
Now old Man cries a young Boys tears.
He'll cry alone, adjust, atone,
as he frees subconscious from it's night.

I started writing from my raging fury and pain with Eisenhower's revelations released after forty-some years in secret files. I ended my writings loving two small Korean Children I'd known less than an hour.

These Children have stayed with me, first thru nearly fifty years of emotional torment, and now thru the emotional acceptance of Love. Is it Gods hand? I do not know. ————— *jimmie joe*

A Song of David

The Lord is my Shepard, I shall not want, his prayer began as the artillery barrage increased.. he makes me lie down in... the first piece of hot jagged shrapnel begins its journey thru the young Warriors arm entering his rib cage.. **green pastures, he restores my soul..** the second piece of shrapnel enters just below the aorta and above the liver.. **Ma' Ma.. thru the valley. shadow of** death.. The prayer was finished across the Veil in Heaven; Gods caring arms now enfolded our Friend, our Comrade, and our dead.

The Warrior who wanted and tried to believe was, by the very act of trying, accepted into Heaven by our Loving God. The Warrior like millions before him and after, friend or foe, will not spend eternity in hell. God would not create Humans only to cast most into the pains of hell, what pray tell would be the purpose of such creation?

This I must believe- *jimmie joe*

2

The Wall

The Vietnam Memorial is nearly sacred in my mind, it causes sorrow to well up in my heart that is far and above any other memorial, book, movie or any thing I have felt in this world. The Vietnam Black Wall of Honour seems to hold an aurora of Spirits that are to me tangible.

Those Spirits are there for us, they heal us, be we Vietnam Vets, Korean Vets or any combat Vets. It is a wondrously unique and therapeutic oasis for the hidden recesses of a pained soul, a soul who has lived the reality of a war zone and survived, survived to discover his war didn't end with his return from battle. We all need an oasis such as the;

"Black Marble Wall".

> *jimmie joe*
> *fishhook junction, alaska*

My shoes will fit most Grunts, some will be pinched and some will walk right out of them. Some will have Ghosts and no shoes, I'll try to lend them mine for a short while, mine are broken in and without the blisters of nearly fifty years. If some writings hurt and cause tears my Friend there is a need, if not? That's great.

bear with me friends

Some emotions I may not express well, many times I will repeat thoughts or feelings, in the beginning this was neither written as/nor intended to be a book. Many of these writings are a series of distraught emotions unwrapped from time, they fell out quite well mixed in their own right, some words just seemed to drop from my mind onto the paper without thought, rhyme?, nor reason.

I was never adept in English class, most of the time I was skipping school and going fishing with my dog "Old Gent". Between all that school skipping, hunting, fishing bluegills and joining the Army at the end of the tenth grade, it's a bit amazing I can read or write at all. I ask your patience with that which I attempt.

3

A glimpse of maladjustment

In Korea about a week before our rotation date we would be pulled off the front line to the comparative safety of Co. Hq., I remember that, I don't remember saying goodbye to my Buddies. I remember going to Japan, stripping naked, going thru the delousing shed and having my body sprayed with DDT to kill the white body lice. We could have any food we desired; I had steak and milk, milk, milk. The Red Cross gave us cigarettes, donuts and whatever else they had. I've heard some say the Red Cross charged the GI's; there was never any charge I had seen.

We sailed to Frisco, rode a bus to Fort Ord and I caught a plane to Chicago the same night. The departure of the plane was held up for us and as I boarded I overheard a civilian complain about holding up the flight for a bunch of damn GIs, these were the first words I heard from a fellow American. This was my introduction to how some Americans felt about the Korean War veterans. I could care less at the time, I had survived and I was home. I could now live out my life in peace. I was wrong, it would be nearly fifty years before my last battle ended and peace took hold.

I can remember flying over the Rocky Mountains and having the euphoria of being alive and going home. Something happened between there and Chicago, I lost my remembrance. I don't remember landing in Chicago, how I traveled from Chicago to Lansing, Michigan or if anyone met me. I don't remember meeting my family, friends or much else on my thirty-day furlough. I remember being at Ft. Jackson, South Carolina but not how I traveled there. For some reason my mind had/has blocked all that out, I've tried and tried to remember but I cannot.

October 1951, Ft. Jackson, South Carolina, about two months after my return from Korea.

Page, 239

Spent time in Army hospital there,
the world twisted not quite real.
I'd developed tunnel vision, was a scary way to feel.
Sights and sounds were far away.
Quite confused in bed I lay.

4

After a short rest the symptoms disappeared and I was released, the Doctors couldn't find the cause. Our recognition of posttraumatic stress would not evolve for decades. I thought it was just I, thru the next forty-seven years I would be adjusting to my non-adjustment. The years 1951 to 1956 were the most difficult, thru the years that followed I managed to slowly placate and veil most of that which distressed my mind. Thru all this time, in my ignorance, I thought I alone carried ghosts of war, I alone was not quite man enough to cope, I alone held back tears, I alone went into hiding. I was not alone in being so wrong.

My memory is fine through the time I spent training my platoon at Ft. Jackson, South Carolina, while on maneuvers in Texas and my discharge June 10th, 1952 from Camp Atterbury, Indiana. It was only during my furlough and time at home where memory has failed me.

I don't remember asking a Lady to marry me and only vaguely remember the wedding ceremony on December Twenty-ninth, nineteen fifty-one. I do remember consummating the marriage; amazingly my memory of forward time remained excellent thereafter, altho I still have the voids in memory of my time on furlough.

There were many insensitive, ignorant civilian asses wanting to know what it was like to kill a man and other kinds of stupid questions, my stomach muscles always twisted tight, I didn't like it. After while I would either not respond or tell them I worked running a PX, that didn't impress them much and they let me alone. I have Grandkids who, 'til my book, never knew I was in the Army let alone in combat.

I learned well how to hide and keep my thoughts from the questioning world outside my head but I couldn't escape the pop-up demons stored inside. I coped by neither talking about nor discussing the demons lurking just below the surface, and in truth in those years my family and friends would have had even less reaction than my family did when I tried to talk about it in January of nineteen-ninety.

The Veterans Administration in early years had no concept of the pain their Veterans *may* have carried unless we became so severely dysfunctional we had to be put away, and once they got you I'm not sure they did any more than drug the hell out of you to keep you manageable.

I was able to work, raise my family and function quite well but there were always pop-up background snapshots in my head, keeping me on guard and depriving my mind of lasting peace. I had left Boy abandoned on his distant battleground, imprisoned by me and exiled to the dark arena of a Warriors mind where Friends and Loved ones may not trespass. This arena of desolation is where Boy must live so the outside world will never know he is not a real Warrior, he's just a little Boy who needs to cry.

Moving to Alaska was almost like going back to the freedom of my childhood. My demons, while still there, became muted a bit and were nowhere near as demanding and constant. Alaska was to a large degree like coming home, I had peace when working in the "Bush" and while hunting, catching fish in places wild and the pure joy my heart absorbed when my Children were young.

My demons were very nearly anesthetized my first twenty-five years in Alaska, they put few demands on me until about a year after I retired and the last of my Children left home in 1985. Increasingly, thru the next five years, I became my vengeance, without awareness I was in a life or death struggle, with deepening awareness I was lost.

jimmie joe,
fishhook junction, alaska

An old Dogface Sarge Wonders
The Two Koreas and a civil war

Let me begin by stating irrevocably I was/am for our intervention into South Korea to stop aggression by the North Korean Army. Our pushing to the Chinese border I now deplore, as it is apparent from declassified papers our leaders knew we were running high risk of war with China. Let me also state, true or not, I believe Mac Arthur coveted said war to free Asia from communism. In total millions of civilians died from massacres, disease, and starvation and with three years of our intensive bombing in North Korea, sadly the starvation continues to this day as the result of a totalitarian government that will not bend.

China entering the war in late 1950 made it not winnable without conquering China. We had politics at the start, politics in the waging and politics at the end. Politics of wars prevention should be politician's obligation; the politics of peace will be the prize.

An Infantryman will never be an expert about the war he is involved in fighting, his area of expertise will be confined to his immediate front, left and right, all else will be rumors of unfounded information, some true and some totally false. I've done my best to write as I remember but with the passage of time I may have retained some rumor as my truth. My deeper poems will reflect my truth.

I have studied the history of the Korean War and formed opinions teeming with questions of truth about some Generals, Politicians and Americas peoples after WW II and well past the Vietnam War. Some opinions are carved in stone some are not. They are my opinions as I try to understand my homelands peoples, be we at peace or war; this has now become a small but vital need of mine. Our past freedoms rest with our Veterans and our war dead, our future freedoms rest with us the living. We have an obligation to uphold those freedoms for which men died.

Korea was the first war we didn't win; Vietnam was the first war we lost. It was not the Grunts who tied or lost, our Buddies, our blood and our nightmares of carnage are spread throughout those bloody lands, from the frozen mountains of North Korea to the steaming jungles of Vietnam we paid the price of wars our countrymen couldn't care less about. Our politicians sent us to battle and with disdain denied us our victory. Our countrymen denied us our welcome home. Our WWII Brothers denied us accomplishment and our homeland denied us our healing We walked quite alone with only the silence of our dead for decades.

Korean Veterans were totally ignored as they trickled home thru rotation, there would be few bands to meet the troop ships, few parades at home and very few would even recognize us as having been at war, coming home, for some, became "a bridge to far".

Our Korean War prisoners of war released in 1953 were treated with disdain at best because a few succumbed to Red Chinese brainwashing. Our own military and politicians would hint of disgrace on all POWs because of those few, a sad commentary on Americas understanding, caring or loyalty to those who defended her and a sad commentary on this Veteran who came home and hid from war.

Four percent of Americans taken prisoner by the Germans died in captivity, twenty-six percent of Americans in Japanese P.O.W. camps died and a minimum of forty-nine percent of American POWs in Korea died in the camps. The percentage nears an abominable eighty percent if there were any way to obtain numbers executed just after their capture or not reported as Prisoners of War, this would take in most of the 8200 MIAs in Korea, a huge number considering the area of Korea and it's terrain.

Vietnam Veterans were treated with hate by many of our countrymen, mainly by the young people. We force young men to go to war then we shower them with hate! What the hell kind of crap was that? In the end I must leave that to my Vietnam Brothers, I will touch on Vietnam occasionally due to the respect I give the Grunts who fought that bloody war and the anger I retain at our governments and the flower children's treatment of them.

We will never win a protracted ground war without the full support of the American people. A "Just Cause" will have support and is vital to what we profess as free peoples. Callousness to Human life could doom us as a free country, be they the innocent of some foreign land, a Congress that will not reign in a President who uses our military for his own ego or where diplomats are not used to prevent or stop a war. One man can wage war for 60 days without congressional approval. It's insanity! The war powers act is a very great threat to our democracy and must be rescinded. Under our Constitution only Congress has the power to declare war. Only Congress can fund and see to a well-equipped, well-trained modern defense system. Congress can keep us free or cause freedoms demise, a grave Constitutional obligation that is meant to keep us from unjust aggression against other countries or, God forbid, against our own population, it can happen. Waco and Ruby Ridge? Remember our people's reaction? A just cause?

HYPERLINK: <http://www.waco93.com/">

Army troops occupying Japan lacked training in close air support, none in guerrilla warfare, and little training in tactics. We need constant training and a well equipped modern military in a world at peace, if not America will have thousands of extra body bags in Flag draped coffins showing up during the first few months of future wars.

Peacetime is when Congress should have been backing us up with the best of unit cohesiveness training and arms. To back us only after we're in a conflict has been/will be Congresses donation to the death of thousands. Incompetent political leaders have caused the filling of far too many body bags and amazingly no one has ever held them responsible.

In the first few months of Korea our outnumbered, outgunned, ill equipped and under-trained occupation troops were sent into combat to slow down and stop a modern, Soviet equipped and disciplined North Korean Red Army. They had the best of training, tanks and equipment. Their cadre had fought the Japanese and helped win China for the Communists, they were battle-hardened troops and had the cause of "their Civil War". American Troops had no defined cause, no saving our homeland from a tangible enemy. Honour, Duty? We went, we died and the Gold Stars in Moms windows at home were made of tarnished tin.

Equip an ill-trained Army with out-dated, worn-out equipment, pathetic communications and for a while you will end up with chaos. Men tried and died trying, so many lives lost because the Generals, starting from Mac Arthur on down, were complacent after World War Two.

Duty was an eight to five job, then home to your shack-up. Life was easy. Times were good. DAMN but we were so young and those Japanese GIRLS were so great!

President Truman and Congress would not allocate funds for modern, well-equipped and well-trained armed forces. Our leaders and politicians, who should have known better, shirked their duty to our country and the men they ask to defend her. They did more than shirk their duty; they betrayed those men they sent to battle with overly worn radios who's batteries would not hold a charge making communications between units nearly impossible, armaments leftover from World War II and an ammo reserve of about a month. There was no excuse for the lack of equipment and proper cohesive training in unit tactics or physical conditioning They signed a death warrant for many young GI Joes.

With the lead-time prior to WWII troops at Pearl Harbor and the Philippines were ill prepared. In Korea nothing changed, again men died needlessly, we didn't learn. We saved a few dollars in exchange for the lives of our young inexperienced servicemen. These men should not have died because of overly zealous budget cuts put in by congress, they should not have died because the Generals did not demand they be well equipped and trained and they should not have died because of poor intelligence.

If we must send young Boys to war let it be in a well-equipped, well-trained cohesive fighting unit, fighting for a cause that is "Just". Anything less is a betrayal, not only by our politicians and Generals but also by the American peoples. They elected the damn liberal politicians who disdain the military vocally and monetarily until disdain becomes need, need becomes death, death becomes clay, clay becomes grass and a Mother kneels and cries for a Son who, with training, may have lived.

Where the OSS/CIA was and what they were doing I have no idea. They certainly had not been doing their job else they would have known about the massive buildup of North Korean troops prior to June 25th. 1950. Sadly I'm not too sure some didn't know.

Young American Boys now paid the price for politicians and Generals who rested on their laurels after winning the BIG ONE and did nothing to assure our winning the future "little wars". They did us, who must defend America, a great disservice and were the cause of death for thousands of young Boys. On the job training for combat is not what our Armed Forces should be about.

We learned but it was quite gory. We had the North Koreans pushed to near the Yalu River (Chinas border with North Korea) in November 1950. We'd won! Home for Christmas! Home to my Helen! Home to my dog "Old Gent"! Not quite! First us Grunts must deal with the results of an insubordinate General, a President who catered to him until it was to late and a Congress that had no balls to live up to their Constitutional duties. *Hell I doubt if most in Congress ever read our Constitution, our Bill of Rights or listened to their own oath of office.*

Us Grunts are those who pay the price
when Politicians do not try.
Us Grunts who don't amount to much.
Us Grunts; The ones who die.

There were prior warnings from our men to Mac Arthur of Chinese troops among the dead, which he ignored. The Chinese warned our State Department not to put our Army on her border, another warning ignored. There was no attempt by Congress or our diplomats to reign in Mac Arthur before we reached Chinas border. There was total failure by all politicians and the State Department, a series of fatal decisions that would cost the lives of several million more humans, including thousands of young Americans.

The "home by Christmas" promise was not to be as we were rather busy with hoards of Red Chinese regulars. Mac Arthur's ego and politicians malfeasance extended the war another thirty-two months. All of Korea and our troops paid heavily for our "trusted" politician's gross blunders. At the best our Generals and Politicians egotistically misjudged China's paranoia of a foreign power at her border, at its worse it was to test the mettle of Communism.

Mac Arthur knew the Oriental mindset better than any Caucasian alive, I feel he knew damn well China would respond to our troops at her border. His last great campaign would be to free China from the communists. His military mind dictated he could and should save Asia from Communism; his assurances to Truman that China would not enter were blatantly false.

Chinese Regulars attacked the Marines in northeast Korea in October of 1950 than withdrew for no discernable reason except possibly to show they were serious about us staying back from her borders. At this time diplomacy should have taken over, the war would have ended with well over 3,000.000 lives, mostly civilians, saved. The political decision to battle for the complete reunification of the two Koreas came at a cost in lives only politicians would be willing for others to pay, a cost borne mostly by the Korean civilian populace.

You're right we didn't win. We tied; the ones who lost are in the ground, the ones who tied came home to a country's total indifference. All our dead young Boys and so damn few cared. Those weren't the best of times. America gave us no acceptance; no have a beer Buddy, no job well done and no rationale for the acceptance in our minds of the carnage one faces in war. Some "Forgotten Warriors" felt no justification for their taking of Life in "Your Forgotten War". Look to yourselves America for ignoring men you send to war, ignoring a reality that will never be yours. It was a crummy vacation. Best we forget it? We tried but wars are never forgotten by those involved, be it the Warriors or the poor Civilians caught up in death caused by the damn politicians. We never forget, for some amnesia would be a blessing.

Our next war went beyond the country's indifference to our Korean sacrifice. Some bastards harassed and spat on our returning battle weary troops. They didn't have the courage to risk jail by spitting on our politicians who approved our intervention into Vietnam's civil war.

Politicians had no concept whatsoever of the "cause" of the Viet Cong and the Vietminh and committed the vast numbers of ground Troops to do what no army had been able to do for God knows how long. The Vietminh had fought the French prior to WWII, the Japanese during and the French again after WWII. Now they were fighting us. The ignorant mind-set of this cold war period could not comprehend there was a vast difference between a war of nationalistic unification and Communism's world threat. We sent men to die for all the wrong reasons plus no support at home. Again we never stood a prayer of victory because of politics at the start, politics during and politics at the end.

Politician's get real stupid as they beat the drums of war, when they finally figure out the cause is wrong they still continue, a damn shame. I give you President Johnson's lie; the 1964 Gulf of Tonkin incident was his Big Lie, a collaboration of our top brass and President Johnson. A set up to submit to Congress so approval could be obtained for the huge build-up of ground troops, a boost for Johnson's ego as the war wasn't going well. Again a few million more Humans would die including many thousands of young Americans.

The Tet offensive caused Johnson not to seek re-election in 1968; he didn't want to go down in history as the first President to lose a war. I mention Politicians quite frequently in my writings, always in anger despairingly spun from history. Something has been quite wrong when presidents so easily commit us to wars and Congress rubber-stamps its okay in the name of backing us up.

The Civilian dead outnumbered Americas dead well over 60 to 1 in Korea and Vietnam. I have a problem with the huge number of innocent who die in war, especially the little Children, life somehow is no longer precious to Americans as long as death is far away and gruesome films don't show up on the evening news too often.

Like most wars the final endings in Korea and Vietnam were political decisions. We have three choices of ending a war, total victory, compromise, or just get the hell out. Politically the latter takes the most courage. Human lives and "saving face" do not equate. Some of our Politicians and Generals egos are pure bullshit, along with their hearts, brains and thoughts. War to some is a game played out thru pawns that must protect the Kings image at all costs. I submit millions of innocents may die but winning, right or wrong, is why they play their game.

Nearly every Infantryman exposed to enough combat time, with shifting battle lines, carries one or two Ghosts of dead or dying Little Children and/or dead Buddies, Ghosts that will not leave. The effects or degree of pain will vary but it's there, for some a lifetime. Writing these lines was necessary for myself, now they are for all that carry visions of a war that somehow never quite seemed important to America, wars that bloodied our souls a bit, wars we carried in the silence and pain of limbo for far to many years.

Young people will learn cold hard facts in history books, they will not learn of War. Only those who lived thru them can describe wars, the men who fought or the Civilians caught with their homeland at war and there is no other valid picture. Historians and politicians will do the painting but they are colorblind to the uselessness, pain and reality of war. They may or may not add the true facts building up to, causing and ending a war; their ineptitudes are historic classics.

These lines are not for the bastard politicians who have betrayed our Warriors, a not uncommon occurrence; they merely stamp their betrayal "secret" for fifty years. Political expediency at its best is sealed in our nation archives, those "secret" files.

As for you loudmouths on your barstools, those who say "hell man that's war" to cover any incident, those who brag of their killing and those who have never cared, I ask that you please not read my writings, to such as you they will mean nothing.

I now to speak to our Christian Brothers, since our revolution we have sent young Boys into battle, first to earn and than retain our Freedoms. If our Lord had not yet sought them out, or they had not heard, or did not answer, is their fate eternal Hell as they die in battle? There have been over one million who have died in our wars, we demanded the lives of these young men in the name of Freedoms we retain. Was the price many paid their lives plus eternity in Hell? Their sacrifice is not of great significance to most of us, it was vital to those who died, those who died defending your Freedoms.

How do you/we justify sending young Boys into this hellish aspect of dying? The chance of our hearing "Gods Call" exponentially raises as we age, our young Warrior dead do not age. You who send our young to war before the Holy Ghost has touched their Hearts and Soul, you who's words would condemn to Hell those Warriors not "Saved" or "Born Again", yet you accept their deaths as your right. Nay, you have and will demand the sacrifice of their lives/souls as protectors of your Freedoms.

You who are so sure of your place in Gods Love leave some seekers adrift in fear. I believe the bridge you lay out between man and God is exceedingly narrow. God would not build a path so few could find or trod. God's path will hold all seekers of His light. Your narrow path is a torture of Man and a disservice to our Gods Love, Wisdom and Compassion. I, as a seeker, believe you wrong us.

And, we still fought on
From; Page 74

> I know one thing I'd like to feel,
> that God and Heaven both are real.
> But saying I believe won't do.
> Why did our God answer you?

> We seek the calm of sureness,
> a knowing of our Lord.
> We're at fault if we don't find Him
> fore we die by bloody sword?

> Are we to lacking to be worthy?
> Why can't we feel God in our heart?
> I prayed for God but could not find;
> I just couldn't find the start.

Chaplains didn't have my answer,
I must put finding God on hold.
A young Warrior in Gods wilderness,
fights on thru stench of summers death
and frozen dead in winters cold.

Fights on with death around him.
No thoughts of Heaven nor of hell.
Fights on with mind in limbo.
Where will my soul now dwell?

In pain and mire our life runs out,
you gave us death before our time.
We'll never know what God's about?
Our soul now burns? You share this crime.

jimmie joe

War is hell only if you care.

The time has come to begin the task of expressing fifty years of
suppressed and emotionally anguished thoughts held in check far back in
the recesses of my mind, I shall free them.

Page 136, "Tears of rain"

Us who now live please do forgive,
we've let freedoms slip asunder.
We need you friends, dead Warrior friends,
unleash your cannons' thunder.

Bring all your dead, make us all dread
we caused your country's' fate.
Show us life's blood, wounds mixed with mud,
show "Freedoms bloody mate."

****

Just a few poems of my thoughts
from times long in the past,
of Love and War and Little Children,
some stay and some don't last.

Poetic license was used at times
but the truth as I retain.
Tho emotions were tough to express in rhyme.
They became my healing pain.

I know in certain poems I wrote
my pain flowed out as tears,
"twas quite unpleasant typing them,
my Shadow Ghosts from warring years.

There is no joy in my writings,
in war there can not be.
The ones who suffer most from war
are the displaced refugees.

Some non-combatants sit back here
so knowing all and smug,
they've never held a dying Child
who's hurt too bad to hug,

Nor held a dying Buddies hand
while terror thru him flowed.
They seem to think that war is grand.
Thank God I don't explode.

They've never had to kill a man
who's a boy as young as you.
His hopes and dreams are just the same.
His loved ones grieve him too.

16

There is no glory, only pain
in what we do and see.
You loudmouths on the barstools
all get contempt from me.

If you're the type who brags of war
or the people you have killed,

it's best you stop your reading now,
by my lines you won't be thrilled

There are no glorious battle tales,
no courage like John Wayne.
Thru tortured writings by the Man,
Man exorcised the ghosts of war
and neutralized the Boys stored pain.

My two small Children play in peace
in Gods land beyond the sky.
Nurtured thru Love from Soldier Boy.
The "Boy" who choose to die.

jimmie joe,
fishhook junction, alaska

Politicians in war devour their young
and quench their thirst with Mothers tears.
Only the vanquished foes are hung
but all sides fulfill a Mothers fears.

i begin

Boys journey's was long, he was given no map, no compass, no directions and I had a great deal of trouble locating exactly where Boy was hiding. I searched behind the many walls Boy had built, the last wall was a son-of-a-bitch to break thru, I didn't want to enter, I was afraid to enter, but the courage came and thankfully I broke thru.

I took Boys hand and we began unwrapping time thru these pages, while unlocking Boys tomb of pain I wept. As I shed tears Boy had stored for nearly fifty years my journey took me thru his distant maze of time and sorrow. At some point I found I could not release Boys Hand, I was trapped into finishing I knew not what. I couldn't stop until "Little Children—Grown-ups War" appeared in the last room of a young Soldiers tomb of pain. Opening it was tough, really tough. My journey from the mists of fifty years begins, take my hand my Son, we're going Home, we really are.

I never knew him as a man

The following poem is dedicated to the veteran, who in some shadowed area of his mind senses the loss of a small but vital part of himself, a part left on his distant battleground, a part that's his alone, a part unshared, a part protected.

Probably a result never anticipated is we, who faced our enemy in real battle, would be fighting him in our dreams at night for several years and facing Boys flashing images in day for most of our lives, images that keep us from a peace we don't quite find. We constantly push the images back, shun the Boy who left us in bloody battle yet subconsciously search for him, some for a lifetime. We need him home, to touch his pain, to let him know we're sorry and convince him, "it's okay Son, we're home", it's over, it's really over.

jimmie joe

I never knew him as a man

I don't know where he went.
I knew him well tho as a Boy
and the dog we called "Old Gent".

This poem I wrote for a young man,
one I didn't get to know.
I knew him only as a Boy
from fifty years ago.

I remember Boy from Childhood,
he was just a little Lad.
He kind of stuttered when he talked,
nooo — I'd say he stuttered bad.

When Boy was five a little puppy
came to be his pal for life.
When he was feeling sad or hurting
"Old Gent" smoothed away Boys strife.

"Boy and Gent" seemed star crossed Buddies
and I alone would see,
with "Gent", Boys stutter disappeared,
with "Gent", Boys words flowed free.

That fine dog we called "Old Gent"
formed a sacred bond with Boy.
They roamed the woods and fields together
and life became their special joy.

They would wrestle on the front lawn
and cut-up all about the farm,
spend summer days a fishing bluegill
in the lake beyond the barn.

Boys stutter nearly ceased to be
along with shame from teasing days,
"Old Gent" stayed there beside the Boy
and helped Boy thru his stuttering ways.

"Old Gent" finally cured Boys stutter,
then Boy talked like you or me.
That old Dog was really something,
how'd he set Boys stutter free?

I'd like to think God sent "Old Gent"
to that childhood friend of mine,
to love Boy down that stuttering road
and guide Boy thru that curious time.

"Boy and Gent" hunted the field mice
and rats and snakes were fun.
Later on was pats and rabbits
when he'd learned to use a gun.

Boy built huts around the woodland
made with spruce boughs and saplings bent.
They'd always share the game together,
Boy and his dog we called "Old Gent".

That "Old Gent" was something special,
I wish I had a dog like him.
I still can see them both together
but what will be is not what's been.

I remember Boy from high school,
he was kind of like a chum.
He was not inclined to studies.
I was quite sure he'd be a bum.

I was even surer of it when Boy quit school in the tenth grade, not
once but twice. The tenth grade was the last year of high school Boy
finished; he did get to play basketball those three years. Boy was sort of
dumb about some things but he caught up.

He was in on all the high school sports,
basketball his favorite game.
His hands were quick, his feet were fast,
"flash" became the Boys nickname.

I think I sort of liked him,
he grew on you after while.
He had a laughing sparkle in his eye
and a slightly crooked smile.

Boy skipped school to hunt the whitetail,
hunting deer to him was fine.
His biggest love was still the fishing
for fat bluegills on his line.

He skipped school a lot for fishing,
of course he took along "Old Gent".
Their life was peaceful carefree days,
much wasted time they spent.

I shared in all his boyhood pranks
and there were quite a few.
I hung out with all his Buddies
and that fine dog named "Gent" too.

He poached the deer in numbers great,
he was devious as could be.
The game wardens couldn't catch him.
Boy was sneaky, Boy was free.

January 15, 1949

He joined the army at eighteen,
I kind of tagged along.
We trained in mud and grime of Infantry
and life still sang Boys youthful song.

Boy's orders for occupation duty with the 24th. Infantry Division in Japan was cut in May 1950. Boy began a 30-day home furlough the first of June where he met his lovely Helen whose essence still resides in Boys heart.

When our eyes met we couldn't pry
our eyes apart, they're stuck!
We didn't even want to try;
Can Cupid run amok?

Boy didn't know 'bout Cupids charms,
he was a bit naive.
Quite soon he'll hold her in his arms
and Boy will "Boy" believe!

That furlough's where Boy fell in Love,
the first love of his time.
The Love would last throughout Boys years,
unconsummated as rare wine.

Twenty-fifth of June 'twas on that day,
A day that changed Boys life.
The North Koreans stopped Boys play.
Boys darling Helen will not be,
will never be Boys Wife.

Boy was a Lad of nineteen years
when we were sent to fight our war.
His mind of pain and death was clean,
it would change forevermore.

They shipped us out together
'cross that ocean wide and wild.
I was to become the fighting man
and Boy remained the Child.

(**bold** type denotes "Boys" outfit)

The U.S. forces at Mac Arthur's disposal included the four divisions in Japan—the 1st Cavalry Division and the 7th, **24th**, and 25th Infantry Divisions. Due to Congressional budget restraints the divisions were lacking over a third of their infantry, artillery units and most their armor units. Existing units were far under strength. Weapons and equipment were war-worn relics of World War II and ammunition reserves amounted to about a month's supply.

None of the divisions had reached full combat efficiency, hell they weren't even close since cohesive unit training had been scandalously neglected. The men had no idea of how deadly this lack of training would become. Occupation duties seemed to be all Mac Arthur was concerned with, to me this was dereliction of duty. Pre-WWII in the Philippines and Hawaii also faced the real problem of being unprepared and many died needlessly, we court marshaled a few Admirals for Congress and Roosevelt's malfeasance of not funding the military for years. General Mac Arthur escaped without charges.

> The rhymes below are not about the dying,
> nor the dead we left across the sea.
> They're to show a young Boy trying
> to cope with wars insanity.

> We headed north from Port of Pusan
> on a bullet riddled train.
> Boy and I crouched alone in cattle car
> as fear wafted across Boys brain.

> As Boy rode the train to our assignment
> with the **24**[Th]. that day,
> he thought of God and death and dying.
> God don't let me be a coward,
> please don't let me run away.

> Boy answered now their bloody battle calls,
> Politicians failures cause wars pains.
> Boyhood fades in ancient mists of war,
> soon I the Man must take the reigns.

We had intelligence data from several sources and should have prevented this war, at the very least we should have been much better prepared. Our Military at all times should be a well trained, well equipped, cohesive fighting force in top physical condition, anything less and we betray those we send to war, we cause some deaths as surely as if we lined them up before a firing squad.

The **34**[th] losses were more than 530 men out of its total strength of 1,549 present at Taejon alone. The leadership losses were horrendous in the regiments they included four regimental C.O.s and two operations officers in just over two weeks. The 1st Battalion lost its executive officer and the **3/34**[th] lost two battalion commanders and its operations officer.

The division commander, General Dean, was also missing in action. {He survived in the hills avoiding capture for about 45 days} General Dean was awarded the Congressional Medal of Honour for action at Taejon.

On July 29, the **34th** was dug in near Kochang. The regiment had no switchboard and was short of mortars, rocket launchers and machine guns. Its commander, Colonel Charles E. Beauchamp wanted to pull his regiment back three miles, but the new division commander, Brig. Gen. John H. Church, ordered him to stand fast. Two North Korean attacks at 5 a.m. cut off Company **I of the 3/34th** and pushed the 1/34th out of position. The 1st Battalion later rescued all but one platoon of **"I"** Company.

About the first of August, the **24th** Division deployed in positions behind the Naktong River on a 40-mile front, with the **34th**, 21st and the Republic of South Korea's 17th Infantry regiments on line from south to north. The **34th's** sector about 34,000 yards, along which were deployed the 493 remaining troops of the **3rd** Battalion.

The average of one man every 300 feet can only be justified by the desperateness of our situation, we should have been wiped out. We were forced to learn by on the job training, I ask politicians to note the price we paid while learning.

We were not tin soldiers; we were flesh and blood and hope. We were and are the past and future dead of uncaring politicians, even tho we live, we've seen our dead who never knew of their betrayal.

The 515 troops of the 1st.Bn. **34th** waited in reserve at Kang-ni, about two miles from the river. The **34th** numbered 1,402 men, less than half the authorized Regimental strength. All three rifle companies of the **3/34th** were scattered in small enclaves and outposts along the southerly bank of the Naktong river.

The regiment was critically short of vehicles, 4.2-inch mortars and, the mainstay of Korean War rifle squads, the Browning automatic rifle. Some 3.5 inch rocket launcher, a replacement for the wimpy 2.76 inch relic of WWII, arrived at Taejon but the effectiveness was miserably lessened due to the troops unfamiliarity with the weapon and the lack of tactical training in its deployment against tanks in a city. Had the troops had this training they could have destroyed every Russian T-34 tank within Taejon, several hundred lives would have been spared in this battle alone and possibly gained enough time for reinforcements to arrive.

On August 4, elements of the North Korean 16th Infantry Regiment staged an assault across the Naktong between Companies I and L, **3/34**

Infantry, and overwhelmed most of their positions. Communist North Korean troops drove about five miles into the **24th** Division sector, bringing about the First Battle of the Naktong Bulge. This eventually involved the entire **24th** Division, the U.S. 1st Provisional Marine Brigade, the newly arrived 9th Infantry Regiment and 1/23rd Infantry (both from the 2nd Infantry Division) and the 2/27th Infantry. The struggle lasted until August 19.

The **34th** Infantry gave every thing it had, Company K stayed on its 7,500-yard front along the Naktong alone until ordered out on about August 14. At the outset, the 1/34th launched a counterattack, but part of Company C was trapped in a grist mill, where the men valiantly held out until rescued. Captain Albert F. Alfonso, with remnants of Companies A, C and L, held a small perimeter at the nose of the bulge until ordered out on the night of August 8-9. Elements of the regiment took part in a number of counterattacks between August 6 and 18.

The **34th** made its last attack on the August 18th, during which Company C was reduced to 37 men and Company A to 61. Company L lost more than 20 men in a few minutes to a counterattack. When it was relieved by the U.S. 2nd Infantry Division on August 25, the **24th** Division numbered 10,600 men—8,000 short of full strength.

Only 184 of the original regimental strength of 1,898 men remained in the 34th Inf. RCT.

On August 27, Lt. Gen. Walton Walker, U.S. Eighth Army commander in Korea, dissolved the **34th**, converting the 1/34th into the 3rd Battalion, 19th Infantry, and the **3/34th** into the **2nd Battalion, 21st** Infantry Regiment. Those who served and survived those first sixty-three days of the war will remember well our politicians years of drastically under-funding our Infantry units.

The **34th**. is a classic, but only one example out of many contributing to thousands of needless deaths in Korea. Deaths caused by politicians' distaste of spending money on research and development, new equipment and intensive unit training during peacetime. Making our military into cohesive fighting units is the obligation of Generals and politicians, not the Grunts.

It's peacetime when Congress must stand behind our military, assure the budget is adequate and demand the units are trained as cohesive, effective fighting units. Again I stress anything less is a betrayal of the young Boys we send to war, a needless death warrant for many. With well trained Officers and non-coms to enforce discipline the terror felt by some Troops would have been eliminated and nearly all panic prevented, the Troops would have known what to expect and execute.

In a larger war young lives will still be lost in the slowing down of a foe while we draft and train civilians, but there will be thousands fewer of Americas young boys dying needlessly and coming home in body-bags as bits of Clay for their Moms.

> T'was along the bloody Naktong River
> that I noticed my Chum change.
> His eyes lost their laughing sparkle
> and his smile was not the same.
>
> Boys conscious mind began to slow
> from sights of man-kinds gore.
> Subconscious mind recorded all,
> enclosed in walls now being built
> by the Boy they sent to war.
>
> Boy thought much about his dog "Old Gent"
> and the peaceful woods back home.
> His dull eyes now hid the numbing sights
> where future ghosts of war would roam.
>
> His Granny wrote Boy a letter,
> said his good "Old Gent" had died.
> His dog. His Friend for all those years.
> He just broke down —— Boy cried.

It was about this time, august 1950, we had a bloody nighttime firefight the end result being three deuce and a half trucks with bodies thrown in filling them to the top of the side racks. I walked on these dead young Boys looking for my Buddies; I didn't find them, they must have been further down than I could uncover.

Walking on our dead did not bother me consciously at the time. I can, right now amazingly, see a few faces. They must have been seared far back in my memory cells, they were never part of my Ghosts, it's odd. I now feel sadness fifty years later.

27

There must be a lot of survival pushed back beyond our brains and I just unwrapped a piece of time from mine. The sorrow is in the youngness, so very, very young; they really were little more than Boys and so many in one night. ... *Lord I'm sorry.*

'Bout then in nighttime battle
or it could have been in day,
Boy just kind of up and disappeared.
He became a different kind of M.I.A.

He would take no more mans warring hell,
that Childhood Friend to me so dear.
One minute fighting stoutly by my side,
then, thru cordites mists, "Boy" disappeared.

I think I tried to find him later on,
maybe for a year or two.
I don't know how or why he disappeared.
Guess Boy and I were thru.

He'd built his walls, he'd built them well,
enclosing Mans demons in the rooms.
While building walls and filling them
the Boy became entombed.

He could be somewhere I won't know
with his dog we called "Old Gent".
Roaming the woods and fields together
as in his peaceful youth he spent.

I still miss Boy just a bit.
Guess I miss his "Old Gent" too.
He bugged out on me in bloody battle,
the Boy I knew so very well
left with the man I never knew.

I'll not know what he might have been,
he would not be shaped by warring time.
His walls absorbed the shaping
and that Boyhood friend of mine.

The Boy who left for war is gone.
He was never seen again.
Only I came home from battles.
Now a stranger 'mongst old friends.

The ground battles all were over
but for years they would remain,
enclosed in walls built by the Boy,
Mans flashing, Ghostly visions
from the Boy entombed with pain.

In sleep Boys walls released the Ghosts,
Ghosts of long repeating dreams.
The first few years I would awake
as lips closed upon Boys screams.

I'd push them back by light of day.
My nightly fight; God make them end.
I grew to dread my nighttime battles.
Always alone; No Comrade Friend.

No Comrade Friend to aid my fight.
No solace my soul could share.
Just I alone in twisted night
and death, not peace, awaits me there.*

The Boy was trapped in self-made tomb
built to protect the Man.
The Man was trapped by social mores.
It took years to understand,
Manly men may cry.

One Boy died, one Man survived
those days so long ago.
One made it into Manhood.
Jim misses jimmie joe.

I kind of hope I get to meet them
in that land beyond the sky.
I'd like to see my dog "Old Gent"
and the Boy who choose to die.

Jimmie joe
Fishhook junction, alaska

My time of twisted nights

In the following repeating dream an artillery round kills me, the dream made no sense. On the nights I had this dream death not only awaited me in sleep, death took me in exactly the same way every time, as in all my repeating dreams, carbon copies every one.

Why repeating dreams that are not real?
Is there reality I won't recall?
Why could I cope in actual war
and in sleep not cope at all?

We are attacking a steep wooded hill in daylight; the trees are just beginning to turn so it must be fall. I sense my Buddies to my left but can't see them due to the thick brush. As we continue up the hill we begin taking machinegun fire from directly in front of me, I twist-pull the pin on a grenade, rear up and throw it. I'll never know if I got the machinegun as an artillery round hit in the same place my body was dropping back down to. My whole world turned into a huge exploding flash of light, I was blown up and out from the hill and felt neither pain nor fear. Even tho I had no body left I somehow emitted a silent primordial scream; I would awake sitting bolt upright in bed as my lips closed on the fading scream I never heard. My wife would hear it and never quite understood, nor did I.

After nearly half a century I still vividly remember the hill, the leaves half yellow and half green, throwing the grenade, the explosion with its huge flash of light and being blown up and out. I have no desire figure why; it's just the way times were for a while.

In this repeating dream half the damn Chinese Army is chasing me along a ridge pockmarked and cratered from artillery. The trees are all snags and stobs from direct hits or airbursts. I am running without a weapon, the enemy is about two hundred yards behind me in a vee formation. In this dream I am feeling fear but I must try to stop them. I come to a dead enemy soldier, pick up his bolt-action rifle, kneel, aim at the lead man and fire. The bullet goes about twenty feet out of the barrel and just falls to the ground. DAMN! I rack in another round, the point sticks in the chamber and the base jams in the magazine; I can't un-jam it so I'm off running again. I go thru the same thing over and over, they never gain on me and it's the same shredded trees, the same craters, I pick up the same rifle and the same formation keeps chasing me for what seems all night. I don't have this dream anymore but the years I did have it every detail would stay exactly the same and as always I was alone.

The following repeating dream has to do with an attempt to rescue a fellow soldier in a bombed-out village; this is the only one I occasionally still have and it started years later then the others.

This dream begins with me kneeling beside a section of wall left from a bombed out building, I am peering around the partial wall looking for the sniper who had just shot a fellow soldier. The soldier is laying face down and appears lifeless in the middle of what appears to be a town square. My eyes are searching the partially bombed out buildings across the square for the sniper when I appear standing beside my kneeling self. My dumb standing self is in plain view of the sniper. The conversation is as follows:

Standing self: Go get him.
Kneeling self: I will.
Standing self: Go get him now!
Kneeling self: I will, give me a minute!
Standing self: You've got to do it and you know you're going to do it. So do it now!
Kneeling self: I know I am, I will in a second.

We argue in this fashion for short while with dummy staying in full view of the sniper. In the next instant I am kneeling beside the soldier with my left hand on his left shoulder, my left knee on the ground and I hold the M-1 in my right hand with its butt on the ground. My head is turned toward the buildings across the square still searching for the sniper, I turn back to the soldier and start to turn him over — the dream always ends there, I never get to see his face or see if he is alive and I remain asleep. This was not a bad dream.

After a period of time, two years or so, I don't recall now, as I merged into the distressing part of my dreams a voice would say, "wake up jim it's just a dream" and I would awaken. The voice spoke earlier and earlier during the dreams, after while as soon as a dream began it would end. This basically ended my long battles while sleeping and my time of twisted nights.

Only one dream had anything to do with my recollections of war, the three other repeating dreams, the ones recorded here, are a blank in my war remembrances.

Except for the dreams about my two small Children (Little Children — Grown-ups War on page 65) I was always alone, only the enemy were alive, the enemy and me. ————— Go figure.

"Boy"

Boy could take no more mans warring Hell,
that Childhood Friend to me so dear.
One minute fighting stoutly by my side,
then, thru cordites mists, "Boy" disappeared.

With no conscious knowledge of Boys leaving
I took his place in battles storm.
All the pain of killing, death and dying
I would accept as man-kinds norm.

I would accept the death of fallen Comrades
with distant pain and zombie gaze.
This pain that always kept it's distance,
taps lightly in life's autumn days.

I've lived a life that's long and full.
I've had a Wife and held my Child.
Great-grandbabies walk thru my heartstrings.
I've caught those fish in places wild.

These wondrous gifts bestowed on me
were from a sky of mostly blue.
Wisps of guilt drift by when I ask the WHY,
why me my fallen Warrior Brothers,
why me instead of you?

jimmie joe
fishhook junction, alaska

Boy's foe

I would accept as sacred duty,
honour-bound,to destroy my faceless enemy.
Their dead we'd strewn throughout that land,
if by chance we looked, with time we see,
most dead were young, —— young Boys like me.

There are no words to express my thoughts on this; I guess I shouldn't have skipped so much school along with the fact of my not finishing high school. Words are so damn inadequate for conveying my feelings. I'm trying to say I'm sorry to the young North Korean and Chinese Soldiers who died by my hand. I do not apologize as the hands of politicians and fate put us together in combat, we did our duty. I had no remorse at the time, no joy, no hate, emotions were muted, a strange world combat. It's a stranger world in which I attempt to express my sorrow to the spirits of men who have been dead fifty years.

My reverent prayer is all young dead of war will be reincarnated, this goes against my Christian teachings but God could do it if he so desired and it is in my prayers God will.

I pray they will know the joyous time of a full life with a true and loving Wife, little Children and Grandchildren to hold their finger as they walk together. May they catch those fish in places wild and live out their lives in peace.

So I say to the Spirits of those whose death I caused, my sorrow is I deprived you of all the joys in living I have known.

I care that you died,

jimmie joe

35

Boy's deep sorrow

I would accept the massacred civilians,
from Babies small thru tired old Men.
All across that "Land of Morning Calm"
lay tortured dead 'mongst slaughtered Kin

"Civil" wars are nearly always brutally vicious, Korea's was exceptionally so. The North slaughtered whole villages rumored to be Christians or American sympathizers; Unknown to me at the time the South Koreans also slaughtered anyone even rumored to be Communist sympathizers. Our top brass, the State Department ect, which must have included the top of the executive branch knew of these massacres. It's a blow to realize ones cause was so corrupted. I never questioned my government's honour, ——————————— I was wrong

Altogether the North and South Koreans massacred tens of thousands for no reason, Men, Women and Children were butchered. Our bombers killed tens of thousands in the north and altogether these added up to several million Human dying in fear and pain. The heavy bombing of cities seem to have become a legitimately accepted type of massacre (collateral damage) starting with World War II.

Dumb, smart, incendiary, cluster or any other type of bomb we can think up and drop on population's centers is a coldly calculated massacre. No matter what nice "collateral damage" type name the spinners come up with the poor bastards are dead. The surviving Children will develop pencil thin arms, legs, and distended stomachs; their hair may turn a bit reddish.

Their eyes, look in their eyes my friend, tell me what you see. I see a little Child who's eyes reflect no light, only the dullness of the dead, our little walking dead, little Zombies of politicians. Death will come slowly, at the end the Grim Reaper will become the caring parent. ....
Damn you bastards....

Americans will continue getting the morning paper, having breakfast and "you know Ma" we blew the Hell out of 'em last night agin, this wars been going on a long time, by God you'd think we'd be runnin out'a bombs wouldn't yu? Oh well. Better get the Kids ready for Church, it's a nice sunny day lets have a picnic down by the lake this afternoon.

I kinda feel like just relaxin, it's been a tough week.

Page 71, October 1950

> Two small Children crumpled by a crossroads
> with no one else around.
> Two casualties of grown-ups war,
> soon little bodies in the ground.
>
> A little Boy of five or six
> with eyes dulled flat from pain,
> held littler Sister near the ditch.
> Her eyes held pain the same.
>
> Leaha's little head was on Kim's chest,
> Kim's arm round Leaha's shoulder fell.
> Four haunting eyes imploring us,
> this is getting tough to tell.

Americans, such as myself, have no real concept of the tragic misery of a war being fought where ones family and totally extended family reside. Some say "well hell ya that's bad but there ain't no rules, that's war ya know ". No I don't know! I do know Americans don't know shit about wars real pain. That includes myself.

A few million more died from the friend and companion of war; Starvation, Disease and sadly, Suicide. Somewhere between two and six million Korean civilians died, no one knows, they guess. Hell few cared and they still don't care. Damn the worlds politicians, the safe, fat, contemptuous, flag waving bastards who consider a crime against Humanity as something only the loser can commit and be prosecuted for. The egotistical asses never contemplated the thought of even considering war itself is a crime against Humanity.

I would accept the bombed-out northern cities
as justice for our enemy.
I would accept the maimed and starving Children
thru war dulled eyes that don't quite see.

To much death gave dead a neutral view
and thus they stayed as years rolled by.
Except two small Children clung to me,
inside my head they would not die
and I would feel the lost Boy cry.

In the nightmare mangles of mans warring
it seems there lurked a cowards spawn,
'cause in fact took nearly fifty years
'fore courage asked WHY Boy had gone.

I would accept without a spoken question
my country's apathy to Boys war.
I would accept while never really knowing
the cause my Buddies had died for.

I would accept Boys flashing, ghostly visions
and never ask or question WHY.
I would accept the damn repeating dreams
and unheard scream when I would die.

I would accept the dead and crippled Children
as "collateral damage" of mans wars.
With Boys resurrection thru my writings
there's no acceptance anymore.**

Politicians sent our Boys to battle
in wars that held no victory goal.
Several million deaths they'll never question,
nor atonement for a Warriors soul.

So for all my living wartime Buddies
and the ones fate chose to die,
forgive me Friends but I must ask,
asks our callous politicians—**WHY**?

jimmie joe
fishhook junction, alaska

**   In retrospect there was never acceptance of "collateral damage", hell the word hadn't been spun yet. At the time my conscious mind was past being traumatized by the sight of Children crippled and starving from our bombing North Korean cities. At this stage of the war we were quite well conditioned to Mans inhumanity to Man thru our earlier battles and the sight of many massacres of Men, Women and Children by the North Koreans.

Flat dull eyes (The thousand yard stare) and muted feelings are Mother Nature's way of letting us function without becoming a section eight, so I say there never was acceptance of the dead, the maimed or the starving. We're given only a temporary hiding, a semi-reprieve so to speak, a partial reprieve till WHY?

For some of us the time comes when we must ask WHY and than examine our war. Our very own war, *you know the one we keep inside, the one that so often appears unbidden, the one that hurts and you don't want to think about but the son-of-a-bitch is part of you and you weak kneed sniveling bastard. Yeh that's the one. Sorry Friend but that is the one.*

We won't know what to examine and we won't know the question but, —— we must answer. My semi-reprieve lasted nearly forty years, when it ended in the fall of nineteen eighty-nine it was only by the grace of God that it didn't end with a very loud bang.

My examination began aboard my boat in peaceful Halibut Cove, Alaska in mid-July 1997. I've found most of the questions and many answers thru the intervening years and the method that worked for me was writing and writing and writing, on paper white with pain in black. It was tough getting long repressed/suppressed emotions dug out and printed where I could see them in black and white, once written down I could no longer push them back behind my walls. The pain and tears flowed as words brought forth daylight from the darkness of the Boy imprisoned.

I would read the writings that were painful over and over 'til there were no tears. The worse by far was the poem about two small Korean Children who didn't make it. I typed over forty thousand words before examining the house of dismay in my brain where those small Korean Children lived. Many times I had told my friends I was finished with my writings, I thought I was. I knew I wasn't.

One morning I drove to Wasilla, picked up typing paper, an extra ink cartridge and for some reason what turned out to be the most important item, a bottle of Jack Daniels. I drove home, set up the word processor, put on my glasses, opened the bottle and began my one fingered typing and one fisted drinking.

I began the unwrapping of a piece of time about a small little Boy and a smaller little Girl. (It's been over three years since I opened that bottle, now writing this part down for you my Friend I have wet eyes, not of guilt or unresolved conflict, the writing has triggered a deep sadness for Kim and Leaha who have somehow, in my heart, become my Children.)

I must have been quite a sight after a few hours, silent tears streaming down my cheeks, my shirt astonishingly wet, fumbling for the letters on the keyboard, wiping my glasses, wiping my eyes, trying to see the keys, and about killing that bottle.

I didn't accomplish much in the writing but I did break thru a wall, it was painful and stayed painful thru the many readings after completion, but it was the key to nearly all. With time it gave me the peace I had cried out to God for in nineteen eighty-nine and some part of my brain may have been praying for much longer.

I retain a sorrow with love when I think of my Kim and my Leaha, I quite believe the sorrow will stay 'til I pass thru this veil of life and enter the land beyond the sky. In a burst of Love the sorrow will be gone and those I've loved, those who have loved me, will greet me. And *two small Korean Children will rush me with arms outstretched for their hug.*

I'm not interested in wars glory,
the recounts I quite despise.
Try telling your war stories
thru my Kim and Leaha's eyes.

The poem "Little Children—Grown-ups War" contained the QUESTIONS, the ANSWERS and the way home from a very long war for a nineteen-year-old soldier Boy.

jimmie joe

Remembered

M-1 rifle upside down,
Korea, 1950 late September.
Fixed bayonet stabbed deep in ground,
I'm one that does remember.

Helmet placed atop the thing
to mark his lonely grave.
One dog-tag on chain does swing,
The name on it reads "Dave".

Between his teeth the other tag
As rain washed blood away,
back then we had no body bag,
no more will Dave and Jenny play.

The rain, this death of late September,
will Jenny understand?
I won't forget, I will remember
when Jenny lost her Davie man.

His Jenny also will also remember
the sadness of this day.
One rainy day in late September
God took her Dave away.

With entrenching tool we dug his grave,
our emotions hidden and suppressed.
Interned in it one Warrior brave,
dying in rain I just detest.

On his back the lad was placed,
his eyelids we did close.
Rain poncho protects his face
and covers bloody clothes.

This Buddy that died in the rain,
in the rain of late September.
Jenny your name was last word said,
he loves you Jenny, I remember.

Graves registration I hope will show
and exhume this lonely grave
and take him home — I just don't know.
A White Cross for Warrior brave?

Throwing earth in seemed obscene,
rain made the earth quite muddy.
Six days from now he'll be nineteen,
Happy birthday Warrior Buddy.

All his hopes and dreams or strife,
in the sixty years he should have lived,
ended here with one short life.
He has no more; No more to give.

Mom and Dad will shed some tears
as with sad times they must cope.
For losing him in his young years
their tears fall down — So does their hope.

Grandkids for them not a one,
'tis sad but it is true.
An only child, an only son.
Their line of life thru time is thru.

True love Jenny he'll not wed,
their plans are now awry.
They'll not share a nuptial bed,
alone at night Jenny will cry.

Children who they might have had,
as they'd planned three months ago,
a child not begot can't call him Dad.
My God he missed his Jenny so.

His Jenny's pain is part of war,
For a while she'll question why,
her country sent her Dave to war
and God let her Davie die.

He sailed here from 'cross the sea
this country to defend.
Now Mom, Dad and Jenny's memory.
So few do care, so few remember,
one rainy day in late September.

I dedicate these rhymes to Dave,
buried I don't know where
and all our Combat Vets in graves.
Not to this land that didn't care.

jimmie joe

The loneliest sight I've seen so far in life was that grave on the treeless barren farmland and us leaving it. I suppose any grave under those conditions would appear as lonely but this one sure has been burned into my brain.

I've prefaced the Following poems with the words to Taps I first heard from a fellow light machine gunner from West Virginia, it was along the Naktong River in 1950. I remembered most of the words and found them in their entirety on the net, therefore I accept them as original as we will get as the words have varied thru the years.

The words from a "1862" Civil War Battlefield
"TAPS"

Day is done.
Gone the sun.
From the lake,
from the hill,
from the sky.

All is well.————Safely rest
God is nigh.
Thanks and praise,
for our days,
'neath the sun,
'Neath the stars,
'Neath the Sky,

as we go,
this we know.

God is nigh.

Small White Crosses
Our MIAs

There are no Crosses row on row
for many Warriors brave.
No Flanders fields, no poppies grow
on unknown far off graves.

The internment of our Warriors
near the death camps of our foe,
will interest very few of us.
Most just don't care to know.

POWs and MIAs,
buried where none can say,
in most cases they won't be found.
A price their loved ones pay.

The loved ones have no place to kneel
beside a small white Cross.
No special ground for solitude
in weeping for their loss.

There is no special place for flowers,
no Cross to bear a name.
We have the tomb of unknown soldier
but somehow it's not the same.

These Warriors names are not unknown,
we know their names quite well.
Why are there no white Crosses
for these men who went thru hell?

No name inscribed in Cross of stone
to show their sacrifice thru time?
Erase them from their homelands view.
Erase them from our mind.

Our national cemeteries 'cross this land
have their rows of Crosses white.
Our Warriors who just disappear?
We leave in darkness of our night.

I've not had a son missing in War,
if so I'd want his Small white Cross.
I'd want my place to kneel and pray.
Alone to weep my loss.

I now speak of our brothers Wall,
with it's names in marble black,
with the names of Warrior dead inscribed
plus those who didn't make it back.

As I observe this wall of honour
and the caring with their pain,
I can feel the Warriors spirits
as they drift across my very soul,
pang my heart, mist thru my brain.

The black marble wall is powerful,
my emotions swell toward tears.
The names inscribed in marble black
are much too young in years.

What spirits do and where they roam
this old Vet cannot say.
'Near sixty thousand names on marble wall?
Somehow I feel an urgent need,
an urgent need to weep and
an urge to kneel and pray.

The tears along the wall infect me,
puts painful turmoil in my head.
It was not my war —— Was not my fight.
Still I feel these comrades dead.

I feel the time they didn't have,
like my dead comrades of old.
Why do I feel those Warriors spirits
who make old memories unfold?

Why do I feel this sense of comradeship
with Warriors not known by me?
It's all the names, dead young Boys names.
They lived a while ——— and then they died.
Tell them our "Freedom's free."

A formation of standing Warriors statues
will never be the same,
they are not true, they cannot be.
What's true is a Warriors name.

A name tells us the Warrior lived,
tells of time that wouldn't be.
Tells of rights we must protect,
proves our "Freedoms are Not Free."

Our dead were not tin soldiers,
our dreams were all the same.
Do not give us statues.
Damn it give us our Buddies names.

jimmie joe
fishhook junction, alaska

Our Warriors Without A
Small White Cross

8,177 MIA Tablets
Korea 1950 — 1953

On the Island of Oahu
where eternal summer dwells.
Is a place they call the "Punchbowl"
for our Boys who went thru hell.

Our missing from the Korean War
who's remains could not be found,
have their names inscribed on tablets
in this warm and peaceful ground.

The ground is never frozen
and the grass is always green.
We honour missing Buddies there
in that Hawaiian bowl serene.

There is no stench of summers death,
no grotesque shapes of frozen dead.
But a sad something will remind us,
deep back inside, hid from all view,
old Visions in our heads.

I honour you my Warrior Brothers,
I'll join you in a while.
Will you welcome me as Comrade brave
or will there be no smile?

jimmie joe

Have I upheld your sacrifice and death
as I lived time you never had?
Is our Homeland as Free as when you left?
By "Gods own truth" your answer is ——————?
Your answer friend —————— is mine.

jimmie joe,

50

Those left behind

Those left behind whose tears will fall
on new formed mounds of clay.
They accept the carefully folded flags
on their loved ones funeral day.

They'll accept the flag with tear stained hands
and it never will be said,
the coming weeks or months or years,
the pain, the loss won't leave their head.

The degree of pain will vary
and get less with passing years.
The pain will always be there,
"inside those hidden tears."

Those left behind now pay the price
of the freedoms we retain.
Those left behind are the only ones,
for us a lifetime carry pain.

An exception is the combat Warrior
who survived the bloody land.
I've covered that in other rhymes
and the caring understand.

jimmie joe

"A Small White Cross"
For the forgotten Mothers of our fallen Brothers
1776 —————— thru time

Gods gift to me that morning,
was a fine strong baby Boy.
I held little fella to my bosom
and my heart near burst with joy.

As I breast fed my little fella
our eyes locked tight with love.
He'd always clasp my finger,
my Gods blessing from above.

I helped him with his first steps
and I'd catch him when he'd fall.
Dear God I loved my little fella,
so full of love I 'most could bawl.

I'd walk him to the school bus.
I'd hold his little hand.
Dear God I loved my little fella,
he was his Ma'ma's little man.

He grew up strong and healthy,
six foot two or a bit more.
Dear God I loved my little fella.
Then they sent him off to war.

I prayed for him, oh how I prayed,
I prayed both night and day.
Dear God protect my little fella,
please don't take my boy away.

M-1 rifle upside down
fixed bayonet stabbed deep in ground.
Helmet placed atop the thing,
one dog-tag on chain does swing.

My body's here sweet Mother dear
but my spirit's soared away.
I've left wars hell and I will dwell
with you when we would play.

I'm here with you and Jenny too,
I'm still your little man.
I love you Mom and I'm not gone,
I just came home — left warring land.

God took my little fella
and I'll always question why.
My country sent my joy to war.
My God let my Boy die.

Now I kneel beside Little Fellas Cross,
a Cross so powdery white,
I pray to God, hold my Boy's hand
and hug him extra tight.

Hug him the way I hugged him
in those days so long ago.
Hug him God, really hug him
and my Boy's heart will glow.

Now I see the other Crosses,
a million, maybe more
and a million grieving Mothers.
I had not seen before.

I see the Crosses now so clear,
I can't comprehend just why.
How did I miss those crosses,
'til while kneeling here I cry?

The cross I kneel by's not alone,
there's crosses all around.
All those Little Fellas crosses.
Sons who died on warring ground.

Does my homeland see these Mothers
kneeling by their crosses white?
That mound of earth now's all their worth?
You can't see crosses in the night.

beneath those mounds rests freedoms clay.

jimmie joe

Moms "bit of clay"

About a million weeping Mothers
since our nations birthing day.
About a million tear stained Crosses
placed above Moms bit of Clay.

How quickly we forget our wars
and the white crossed mounds of earth.
How quickly we forget the Moms,
forget their Gold Stars filled with pain.
What can a mound of earth be worth?

Moms loss will lessen thru the years,
it will never go away.
The love they shared throughout His rearing,
a telegram — a bit of Clay.

What thoughts these Mothers do not speak
as we let Freedoms drift away?
Honour?
Honour is now a strangers word
Honour rests enclosed beneath the mound,
enclosed within Moms bit of Clay.

This bit of Clay the final product,
this price of Freedoms holding sway,
from flesh and blood and loving Son, to this,
this I hold in Warriors sacred Honour,
Moms precious bit of Clay.

jimmie joe,
fishhook junction, alaska

"A Small White Cross"
"For the forgotten Daughter's of our fallen Brothers"
1776 ———————— Thru time

Little Daughter, Daddy's Daughter
back when Daddy held her tight.
Little Daughter, Daddy's Daughter,
Daddy was her wondrous knight.

A wondrous knight in shining armor,
she was Daddy's special joy.
Daddy's glad that she's his Daughter,
she's sure glad she's not a boy.

Little Daughter held Dad's finger
after walking time began.
Little Daughter hugged her Daddy.
Hugged him tight — Hugged him again.

Little Daughter missed her Daddy
after Daddy left for war.
Daughter sees her Mommie crying,
what is Ma'ma crying for?

Daddy's death to her means nothing,
not when she is two or three.
She only knows her Mothers crying
'cause Daddy died across the sea.

Little Daughter's just know missing
when their Daddy's not around.
Playing there beside a White Cross,
why is Daddy in the ground?

She'll miss her Daddy less thru time
and Child that is only right.
Time will hide the hurt of Daddy
not being there to hug at night.

Will you believe your God's in Heaven?
Daddy's love is never thru.
You will not hug him, see him, touch him
but he's hugging, loving you.

As she grows into her teen years
Dad's a flitting memory
and I tell you Daddy's Daughter
that's the way that life must be.

Will you believe your God's in heaven?
Daddy watches his girl grow.
Daddy loves his little Daughter,
it's important that she know.

She ask questions of her Daddy's Daddy,
not too often anymore.
'Cause she sees Granddad's eyes misting
when she brings up Daddy's war.

Now she's a Woman fully grown
and tomorrow she'll be wed.
Today she visits Dad's White Cross,
visits Daddy so long dead.

By Dads Cross this Daughter's kneeling
as she talks to Dad that day.
Her mind opens repressed memories
of when together they would play.

Once again she is a small girl,
bouncing, laughing with her Dad.
Bouncing, laughing ———— Now she's missing,
all the time they never had.

For nineteen years the tears don't flow,
tears now flow like a stream.
Tears of anger, love and missing,
Daddy's real, not just a dream!

As the memories flood thru her
a great change will soon come on.
The anger, hurt and missing sorrow,
soon, quite soon will 'most be gone.

Daughter, believe your God's in heaven
now that your heart has opened wide.
Daddy's always loved his Daughter,
He looks on you with love and pride.

Now a peacefulness does soothe her,
her soul is filled with Daddy dear.
She feels Daddy in her heart and soul,
knows always, always, always
her Daddy's always been quite near.

Daddy, tomorrow is my wedding day,
now I know that you'll be there.
Up in front, real close beside me
there will be one vacant chair.

I know there is a God in heaven.
I know Daddy with me abides.
I know the chair will not be empty.
Daddy will be there by my side.

Daughters at a young age losing their Daddies seems to bother me more than anyone else's loss, I don't know why. I feel there can be such a special bond, with the right Father and his "Little Daughter", the feelings of the heart become almost sacramental.

There were no questions of "who am I"?, "Why am I here"?, "What is the meaning of Life"? On many occasions and times that were all to short I knew exactly. Remembering those special feelings of inner peace were a soothing balm, helping me thru my times of turmoil and possibly saving my life. Thank you Little Daughter, Daddies Daughter.

I miss those times. My head and my heart miss those times. Sadly the grown Daughters don't remember that which I find so precious. It is a lonely missing. - dad

jimmie joe

"For the forgotten Fathers of our fallen Brothers"
1776 ————— Thru time
"A Small White Cross"

In Flanders field the poppies grow
beside the Crosses, row on row.

Those rhymes I learned in grade school
in year nineteen twenty-three.
White Crosses then meant nothing
to a small young lad like me.

They drafted me in world war two,
even tho I had a son.
I was stationed on the home front,
I was a lucky one.

Those Crosses placed around the world
meant nothing to me still.
I'd never been in combat.
Never seen the young Boys killed.

We were hero's back on V- J day.
The Country partied 'bout a year.
White Crosses still meant nothing.
I saw no death and felt no fear.

Now I kneel here beside a Cross,
so white in light of day.
Now I kneel here beside a Cross,
'neath it my son does lay.

'Twas along the Naktong River
in far off Korea land.
God took my son at just nineteen.
White Crosses now I understand.

60

I understand the pain they hold,
each and every one.
Forgive me God, I didn't know.
Until you took my Son.

I slowly raise my eyes to heaven,
the White Crosses catch my eye.
Rows on rows of Crosses
and my heart, my Soul does cry.

They stretch beyond this graveyard,
beyond the county, cross this land.
A million small White Crosses.
I beg you God please stop them.
Please God, I understand.

jimmie joe
fishhook junction, alaska

The veil
A Warriors passing

Mom tell my Dad please don't be sad,
I really am alright.
I still reside there by Dad's side,
bass fishing in the night.

I 'm still holding Daddies finger
back when I was two or three.
I'm still riding on Dads shoulders.
I am Love; My spirit's free.

God's gift of life dwells near the veil,
I'm now beyond life's tears,
in a place of peace, of joy, of love.
A wondrous place my after years.

I've passed thru the veil that binds us there,
no more war nor hell from man.
My passage thru our veil was quite okay,
a burst of love was there to greet me
and at last I understand.

This time after my life on earth,
I travel now on rays of time.
I gather joyful stardust from my past,
from those I've loved so very much,
from those I left behind.

My dog "Old Gent'" plays by my side
in this tranquil land beyond your sky.
He radiates our love from Childhood years;
For me, our country's Soldier Boy.
For I've a Soul that did not die.

jimmie joe
fishhook junction, alaska

"Little Children" — "Grown-ups War"

I had no conscious idea of the pain I would endure as I forced myself to start, then complete this poem. My mind was quite protective and possessive of its hidden walls and thoughts of nearly fifty years. It covers my suppressed pain, repressed guilt and a piece of uncharted time. I now unwrap time and tears stored by the "Boy".

At some point I felt a need in my heart to adopt and name two small Korean Children. The little boy is "Kim;" the little girl is "Leaha". As I freed them from my pain, somehow with God's mercy, I've come to love them, the years of distress were much too long.

This was my last poem written while my soul still held the torments of war. After more than forty thousand words my subconscious allowed the walls to break, the tears of a nineteen-year old Soldier Boy to flow. Unlike the tears of Nineteen eighty-nine these were healing tears, tears stored in the silent loneliness' of time. Tears from a Boy held in banishment for nearly fifty years by my ignorance and fear.

I'd received no map to find my way, there were no directions to fall back on and, regretfully, there was no one to ask. The "flash" images of my Korean Children's haunting eyes appearing for all those years as clear as the day my mind recorded them are now gone. I can't consciously recall them, I try and I visualize happy Children holding my hands as we walk in a peaceful land, the fields are green and there is no pain, there is sadness.

The two Korean Children left my conscious mind soon after we'd departed the crossroads in 1950 and didn't appear for over three years. They first appeared in dreams after the Korean War ended in Nineteen-fifty-three. The dreams finally went away but the visions of those four haunting eyes flashed for another forty-six years.

I don't understand why this one piece of time should stand out so vividly thru the years. There were probable a few hundred incidents of civilian, enemy and comrade dead. For some reason my Kim and my Leaha would not leave, they would spontaneously appear inside my head with neither rhyme nor reason. I would run from and try to shun them but never had complete relief until I had written the poem that follows. There were more silent tears shed in this one poem than I had cried in my entire life, they were tears from my very soul. This human's mind is a bit complicated.

I never talked about them; I couldn't talk about them. Putting them on paper was probably the most painful experience of my life. It took all the courage I could muster to finally start and complete these writings about two small Korean Children, my Kim and my Leaha.

> *They didn't train us for aftereffects.*
> *What about our time to cry?*

I know little ones, as I wrote this poem my time to cry had arrived. I cried the tears you didn't cry. I cried tears on your little hands so small and trembling. I cried tears on my inability to do anything to save you. I cried tears on leaving your little sleeping forms to die alone and I cry inside for the years that I fought to ignore and hide your existence. I was wrong. I didn't have the courage to face you any sooner, the path thru the labyrinth was much too difficult, and I just couldn't find my way.

I read this poem many, many times before the tears completely ceased to wet my shirt; the odd thing is I never made any sound, only streaming tears. I now read it with wetness only in my eyes. I feel love for and from my Kim and Leaha, this I did not expect. This I will be grateful for unto the grave and as I seek our Lord, I thank our Lord.

jimmie joe
fishhook junction, alaska

a healing
**

Little Children"— "Grown-ups War"

I'm not interested in War glory,
the recounts I quite despise.
Try telling your War stories
thru our little Children's eyes.

Have you seen the little Children
in our manmade warring lands?
Have you seen their fear strained faces?
Held their trembling little hands?

These rhymes are mostly of my Children,
"Leaha" and "Kim" long in the ground.
Will you adopt some Wars' dead Children?
Mans' made enough to go around.

Will you hold Wars' bleeding children?
Will you help them as they die?
Will you grieve for Wars' dead Children?
In your sorrow even cry?

Tell me it isn't fair to ask you this,
these dumb questions you abhor?
Ask all your favorite politicians
just before we go to War.

Ask about the little Children,
the ones you will never see.
The unnumbered maimed and dying Children,
the ones so far from you or me.

Some of them are Chinks you know,
or Japs, Ragheads or Gooks.
There's Niggers there in Africa
and Spearchuckers and Spooks.

There's Infidels and Sloops and Kikes
and names not known by me.
Worlds' drums of War will always claim
they're subhuman enemies.

.So we'll ignore these little Children,
not quite human, not like us.
We have a name; "collateral damage",
a small mistake, no need to fuss.

Well, I've held collateral damage,
my little Leaha and my Kim.
Multiply these deaths by millions.
Politicians' genocidal Sin.

Have you seen the haunting eyes of Children?
Won't reflect as does a mirror.
Only Warriors there to comfort them
and ease their pain and fear.

Have you seen the Children bleeding
and you couldn't help at all?
Have you held the dying Children?
Damn it! I've begun to bawl.

It's really weird how tears can flow,
near fifty years have passed.
I shed no tears on warring ground,
why now at this long last?

No sound I make but a small lake
forms from these eyes of mine.
I didn't know I would hurt so
typing little Children's rhymes.

This is going to cause myself some pain,
a bit more than I thought.
But I must write of little Children
in that land where War I fought.

Those refugees in miles long lines
trudged thru our lines each day,
there's certain sights so clear to me
like they happened yesterday.

Old men and women in those lines,
little Children by the scores.
Some with Grandfathers and Grandmas,
some left orphaned by mans Wars.

Some Mothers trudged along with them,
little Babies they did hold.
Not one young Dad was sighted,
all conscripted we were told.

This was along the Naktong River
where we made a desperate stand.
Once the refugees got thru our lines
they would be safe again.

These sights were sad, but not as bad
as they'd be when we broke out.
As we sallied forth and headed north
mans' atrocities all about.

68

Dead Babies in dead Mothers arms
by the hundreds maybe more,
Dead Grandmothers and Grandpas.
Grim reaper smiles at mankind's War.

These sights were bad for Warriors young,
in our war numbed minds they'd hold.
They might take years to reappear,
with a vengeance when we're old.

The worse by far were living Children
and their deadened haunting eyes,
The hopeless eyes of little Children
that stay with us 'til we die.

Have you seen the frantic Mothers
as their Babies death draws near?
We may not speak their language
but we cry the same sad tears.

Their anguished tears of pain and sorrow,
all emotions are the same.
Their little Children are our Children,
this slammed home in rhyming game.

I've learned the most from Children's eyes,
the living not the dead.
The painful, awfulness of War
in eyes of Children I have read.

Those haunting eyes I won't explain,
thru life those eyes I see,
I won't discuss those haunting eyes
except thru rhymes by me.

North of Hague, 'mongst farming lands,
along a forlorn and dusty road,
we were moving fast in a deuce and a half
with a heavy ammo load.

Two small Children crumpled by a crossroads
with no one else around.
Two casualties of grown-ups War,
soon little bodies in the ground. *

Stragglers from the North Korean army, separated from the retreating Red Army or guerrillas, would zero their mortars in on crossroads to harass and/or destroy our troops as we pushed their army northward. This harassing fire was probably the cause of these Children's fatal wounds. Why they were all alone I have no idea, it could be their Mother was killed somewhere else.

War is very much more than our young Boys bodies coming home, America has never understood war from the perspective of "their whole family" facing death from bombs, starvation and disease.

All the pains of War are failures by our world's politicians, those nice, safe, fat, and self-righteous flag waving Bastards.

A little Boy of five or six
with eyes dulled flat from pain,
held littler Sister near the ditch.
Her eyes held pain the same.

Leaha's little head was on Kim's chest,
Kim's arm round Leaha's shoulder fell.
Four haunting eyes imploring us,
this is getting tough to tell.

They didn't scream or cry or such,
they never made a sound,
just locked with us their dying eyes
as grim reaper hovered 'round.

Gave them morphine, could not do more,
I held their little hands.
Gave them morphine 'til they slept,
I played their God in warring land.

I do know they slept, if I hastened their death with too much morphine
I just don't know. I had no idea back then I would carry those four pained
and haunting eyes mirrored in my head for most of my life, my secret pain
and hidden sorrow. I pray they didn't awaken except to Gods caring arms
in heaven.

We had to leave them to die alone,
they died alone in sleep.
I knew no way could I atone,
for years my soul would weep.

In this War they were a small sad part
of innocents who died.
Out of several million, just these two
within my soul abide.

These were the toughest rhymes I wrote,
for years I'd fought the visions,
Took many years to set them free,
'twas a needed, painful decision.

I had a little Son who died
in nineteen fifty-four.
My pain was great, but I now state
my Korean Kids hurt me more.

Little Jimmy died a natural death
not from mans inflicted pain.
The mangled dying of those two Children
welded ghosts within my brain.

The only flashback War gave me
and it took 'bout Forty years,
were two Small Children I won't free
'Till I have shed their Tears.

In this flashback my mind seemed to produce, nearly forty years after the event, what appeared to be a physical restoration of Kim and Leaha as they appeared that day in Nineteen-fifty. I dropped to my knees to enfold them before my brain caught up with my arms. While the vision only lasted long enough for me to encircle empty air I was completely caught off guard and my reaction after was one of mild confusion mixed with sadness and a little anger.

My writings somehow have helped me,
after I'd reread them many times.
The guilty pain has left my head,
My therapy thru rhymes.

There is still a sense of sadness
that dwells within my heart,
but we've erased the guilty pain
and Loves' had room to start.

Their eyes no longer dulled by pain,
a sparkle's what now shows.
They walk while holding hands with me,
we walk in summers sunshine
and we play in winters snows.

They are now my little Children
and I'm not a Warrior man.
We walk thru peaceful fields of green,
laughing Children hold my hands.

Of course it's all within my mind,
to my soul it is quite real.
My lines absolved near fifty years
we shared that dying field.

I've welcomed these two Children
to live their lives thru me.
I truly welcome them with Love,
for this Love has set us free.

If you really want to stay,
honest Children it's okay.
I've had you here a lot of years,
in many dreams, thru many tears.

When I find sleep in resting ground
and my soul soars I know not where,
I kind of hope you're still around.
I pray you'll meet me there.

love, daddy

I'm not interested in wars glory,
the recounts I quite despise.
Try telling your war stories
thru my Kim and Leaha's eyes.

jimmie joe

I wish to publicly thank our Lord for letting me live long enough and giving me the courage to cope with the emotional turmoil of completing these painful but healing writings. A nineteen-year-old Soldier Boy has been released from a very long battle against a foe no one had trained him to recognize. "It's good to be home by Golly but who's that old Bastard setting there pecking at that typewriter?"

I don't believe most will understand how events that far in the past can be hidden from the world's eyes so many years then hurt with such intensity when exorcised in print. It doesn't seem quite normal.

The relief I have been given is something I've wanted very much before I died, I am no longer alone with the part of me that never left the battleground. This one poem about my Little Children, my Kim and my Leaha has led to Peace.

Now perhaps I can find that which I seek but for some reason have eluded thru life,

My God

And We Still Fought On

I looked for God on battleground.
I could not find God my friend.
I prayed there with a Chaplain.
No message would God send?

The Chaplain said I must believe.
He could not tell me how.
Picked up my rifle took my leave.
Grannies Hell awaits me now?

There are no atheists in foxholes,
I've heard that since World War Two.
What of us who try but lack belief,
what is our Soul to do?

We seek the calm of sureness,
a knowing of our Lord.
Is it our fault we do not find Him
fore we die by bloody sword?

Does a Warrior have his lords compassion
if he tries to believe in God?
If a Warrior dies in bloody battle
will Heavens peaceful streets he trod?

Does it take more than love and Honour
to walk thru Heavens Gate?
If we feel we've never found our God
will hell be a Warriors tortured fate?

Are we to lacking to be worthy?
Why don't we feel God in our heart?
I asked for Him but couldn't find.
I did not know how to start.

Chaplains didn't have my answer,
I must put finding God on hold.
A young Warrior in Gods wilderness,
fights on thru stench of summers death
and frozen dead in winters cold.

Fights on with death around him.
No thoughts of Heaven nor of hell.
Fights on with mind in limbo.
Where will my soul now dwell?

Will my "Just cause" give Redemption?
How speaks God of my foe?
It's to damn complicated
for this old Vet to know!

I could see Gods stars above me,
they stood out like precious jewels.
My mind was blank 'bout God in Heaven,
could be the blankness of a fool.

What fate awaits me should I die?
Where is the place I'll go?
Will devils laugh? Will Angels cry?
This young Warrior did not know.

If life blood ran out on warring ground
and soaked into stinking sand,
would this fearsome God I hadn't found
take jimmie by the hand?
Say "It's all right Son" I understand?

jimmie joe

the song of david

An intentional repeat.

The Lord is my Shepard, I shall not want, his prayer began as the artillery barrage increased.. he makes me lie down in... the first piece of hot jagged shrapnel begins its journey thru the young Warriors arm entering his rib cage.. green pastures, he restores my soul.. the second piece of shrapnel enters just below the aorta and above the liver.. **Ma' Ma, ... shadow thru** the valley *of death.* The prayer was finished across the Veil in heaven. Gods caring arms now enfolded our Friend, our Comrade, our dead and as eventually You and I.

These Warriors who wanted and tried to believe were, by the very act of trying, accepted into Heaven by our Loving God. Those Warriors like millions before them, friend or foe, will not spend eternity in hell. God would not create Humans only to cast most into the pains of hell, what pray tell would be the purpose of such creation?

This I must believe ————— jimmie joe

The following poem was my first, the title tells you I had no idea where I was going or why. I could go thru and make the flow better and make some thoughts more clear but I won't, when you read this poem I would like you to observe I stayed away from or went around subjects/emotions lurking behind the shadows. Anything not written in poetic form was added later.

76

"A Bit of Wandering"

RA 16 307 188mos 1745January 15, 1949 enlisted in the Army.
Basic in 2nd. Infantry Division., Ft. Lewis, Washington
Desert training 2nd. Infantry Division.
Amphibious training 2nd. Infantry Division, Hawaii
Air transportability training 2nd. infantry Division.

Orders cut in May, 1950 for assignment to occupation duty in Japan with the 34th. Infantry regiment of the 24th. Infantry Division.

"A Bit of Wandering"

Back in May of Nineteen-Fifty
the Army made a decision,
Lets transfer Corporal Jimmie Joe
to the "Twenty-Fourth Division."

That idea was fine with me,
I couldn't wait to go.
I'd never crossed the great wide sea,
but first a home furlough.

For thirty days I'll have some fun
and all that sort of thing,
by chasing Girls in summers sun
to make this lads heart ring.

I met one thru my cousin Jack,
her face I did adore.
She made my heart flip off it's track,
had not been done before.

77

When our eyes met we couldn't pry
our eyes apart, they're stuck.
We didn't even want to try;
Can Cupid run amok?

I reached and took her hands in mine,
them softly I did hold.
Our probing eyes sought out divine
as we viewed each others soul.

Cousin Jack, he kind of stared,
then looked at clouds in sky.
I nor Helen really cared, lost in each others eyes.

We forgot he was around,
did not mean to be rude.
Our limpid eyes they did astound
our feelings and our mood.

Both of us just standing there,
eyes would not break away.
Just holding hands, just holding stare,
I miss it still today.

Almost our eyes seemed to reveal,
a knowing back thru time.
Almost a love, was almost real,
Soul Mate with hands in mine?

Some past life could it be
in a place I know not where,
Helen was holding hands with me
in a lifetime we did share?

.Didn't know then 'bout Cupids charms,
I was a bit naive.
Quite soon I'll hold her in my arms
and Boy will I believe!

While holding Helen close to me,
on my chest her head does rest.
My heart does sing but it's not free,
Those feelings were the best!

It's tied and bound by Helen's charms,
the Charms are ropes of Love.
Entwined with Helen in my arms
I felt peace as Noah's dove.

For two more weeks, both day and night,
a time our hearts did glow.
We walked and talked, held hands, held tight.
My heart just seemed to grow.

I couldn't know in one more week
as love flowed thru my heart,
a war would end what my soul does seek
and forever we would part.

We talked about our future life
and babies, four or five.
How someday we'd be man and wife,
'twas great to be alive.

Twenty-fifth of June 'twas on that day,
A day that changed my life.
The North Koreans stopped our play.
My darling Helen will not be,
will never be my Wife.

That night as we strolled around
in sorrow we did walk.
In sadness Helen's tears flowed down,
to miserable to talk.

This was a sadly painful night
and for life our hearts did yearn.
Let me survive this warring fight.
Please God let me return.

We held each other much, much more,
our hearts mixed love with woe.
It's very sad to leave for war,
ten thousand miles away I'll go.

Just one more night of her warm arms,
we held each other tight.
Just one more night of Helen's' charms,
we held and held all night.

Today I have to catch a bus,
a sad time this has been.
No family there just two of us,
don't let this be the end.

I sailed to Sasebo and then
on to Pusan, my war began.
34th. Inf. Regt./21st Inf. Regt.
24th.Inf.Div. late July, 1950.

A far off land long, long ago,
thru summers heat and winters snow.
The North Koreans fit and trim,
sponsored by Russian Commies,

with commie cadre' discipline.
modern equipped by Russian army.
Blitzkrieged south June, twenty-five,
South Korea won't survive.

So good "ol Harry" used his pen,
which he was quick to do.
The "Twenty-Fourth" it must go in.
Cannon fodder's nothing new.

You must go old Harry said,
or perhaps some other guy.
"'tis better to be dead than red",
dear God don't let me die.

Men in Japan for occupation,
living the easy soldier's life.
Not well trained to fight a nation,
soon must deal with soldier's strife.

So they packed up you understand,
kissed their Geisha girls good-bye.
Guess it's time to be a man,
there, there Geisha girl don't cry.

The "Twenty-First" will join the fight,
have no idea what's ahead.
Left for combat the next night,
two days later near half were dead.

Task force Smith's four hundred men,
out numbered thirty to one.
Only one way the fight could end,
less than one day the fight was done.

Delaying action near Suwan,
Infantry 'gainst commie tanks.
"Bout half the men won't see the dawn.
South Korean monument gives thanks.

What's that the politician said?
Safe at home in USA
These "Mothers children they're not red."
Too young to be a bit of clay.

Dying there in fear and pain,
they'll never see their Moms again.
Nor hold a Wife, nor have a Child,
nor catch those fish in places wild.

They fought thru "Taejon," it was mean,
those ill trained and bloodied men.
In the mountains lost our "General Dean,"
barely slowed the commie war machine.

Just after that out gunned retreat
the Naktong River seemed real neat.
We'll hold them here the generals said,
"'tis better to be dead than red."

That sayings cute in congress halls,
those brave men way back there.
So far from war, so far from death,
bright eyed no vacant stare.

It's hardly cute as it can be
when so many boys are dying.
Ill equipped men of Infantry
'cause politicians were not trying.

My Helen wrote me every day,
love thru her pen would flow.
Her longing, loving hopes she'd say.
Dear God I missed her so.

War was a very lonely place
in that far off killing land.
Her letters let me see her face,
in my mind I'd hold her hand.

None knew when mail call would be,
the front kept shifting 'round.
But always letters there for me,
from this Soul mate I'd found.

Mail call's really quite a treat,
letters from home are super neat,
waiting there with bated breath
until there are no letters left.

The ones whose names they didn't sound
would walk away with eyes cast down,.
they'd set alone and kind of stare
and wonder 'bout their loves back there.

I'd be busy reading mine.
My first love Helen, damn she's fine,
in ten more months if I'm not dead,
when I get home that girl I'll wed.

My heart's so full of lonesome love,
I thank the Lord whose up above.
for my sweet Helen way back there
who keeps me from that lonely stare.

May I explain what letters mean
to lonesome soldiers I have seen?
The letters take us far away
to places where we use to play.

To girlfriends who we tried to fool
around with out behind the school.
To night time bass fishing with Dad.
Want it again, want it real bad.

The only pleasure we receive,
the only thing that will relieve,
the loneliness we feel clear thru,
are letters from back home—from you.

.The "Thirty-Fourth" that one was mine,
I joined them in late July.
As battles raged outside Pusan,
I was exposed to men who die

Twenty miles? and that's not much
Mac Arthur's edict, hold your ground.
The ocean will be the end of us,
we hold or die or drown.

There will be no Dunkirk here
General Mac Arthur said.
Our ships will never rescue you,
hold fast or you're all dead.

That order we did quite despise,
things are not as they should be.
Damn it! real bad we need supplies
if we are to hold our enemy.

Red Army front, Guerrillas rear,
water, ammo and food are low.
Sure wish we were out of here,
we have no place to go.

Slowing commies down was tough,
untrained Boys died while trying.
There's not too many left of us,
a lot of Warriors Mothers crying.

My biggest fear, my greatest dread
and I've just turned nineteen.
Is where I'll go if I get dead,
'cause preachers hell I've seen.

Back at home when people pray
God seems to help them on their way.
Me, God seems to quite ignore,
perhaps it's just this awful war.

Maybe dying? I can't tell.
There's no way I could know.
Spend eternity in Hell?
I'm afraid that might be so.

I know one thing I'd like to feel,
that God and heaven both are real.
Saying I believe won't do,
Why did your God answer you?

Oh! God! I'm scared the young Boy cried,
Sarge I'm scared of Grannies hell!
"I want my Mama" — then he died.
There is much more I need to say,
there is no way to tell.

A repeat;

I now to speak to our Christian Brothers, since our revolution we have sent young Boys into battle, first to earn and than retain our Freedoms. If our Lord had not yet sought them out, or they had not heard, or did not answer, is their fate eternal Hell as they die in battle? There have been over one million who have died in our wars, we demanded the lives of these young men in the name of Freedoms we retain. Was the price many paid their lives plus eternity in Hell? Their sacrifice is not of great significance to most of us, it was vital to those who died.

How do you/we justify sending young Boys into this hellish aspect of dying? The chance of our hearing "Gods Call" exponentially raises as we age, our young Warrior dead do not age. You who send our young to war before the Holy Ghost has touched their Hearts and Soul, You who's words would condemn to Hell those Warriors not "Saved" or "Born Again", yet you accept their deaths as your right. Nay, You have and will demand the sacrifice of their lives/souls as protectors of Your Freedoms. You who are so sure of your place in Gods Love leave some seekers adrift in fear. I believe the bridge you lay out between man and God is exceedingly narrow. God would not build a path so few could find or trod. God's path will hold all seekers of His light. Your narrow path is a torture of Man and a disservice to our Gods Love, Understanding and Compassion. I, as a seeker believe you wrong us.

I hope God took him by the hand
and eased his soul from bloody sand,
held it tight and took him home.
So many deeds I must atone.

Guerrillas round Pusan did roam,
well trained for killing in the night.
Sent a lot of Warriors spirits home
in confusing mixed up fire fights.

The day after the killing stopped,
for some reason I felt no pain.
Trucks filled with bodies to the top,
thrown in back like sacks of grain.

Protecting walls in brain were new,
the reasons why I'll never know.
All those dead were neutral view,
as conscious mind let feelings slow.

Sometime before, not after that,
it took years to understand,
my eyes turned dull or dead or flat.
Conscious mind escaped the killing land.

There is no way I can explain
what takes away the conscious pain.
and stores it way in back of head,
for future times or 'til we're dead.

Subconscious mind can hide away
the sights and pain thru warring days.
As the months or years slide past,
the piper will be pain at last.

Another scene flits thru my mind
winding down those dusty roads,
refugees in miles long lines,
with those loads, back breaking loads.

All they'll own upon their backs,
eyes reflect despair and fear.
Fleeing from the Reds' attacks
only safety's south of here.

Those who think communism is fine,
view those peoples fleeing home.
.Why heading south those tragic lines?
With many children all alone.

Two thousand men in "Thirty-Fourth,"
quite happy in Japan.
'Bout nine July they ventured forth
into that killing land.

Those under-trained troops quite soon would see
as they watched their Buddies die,
the cost of keeping that land free.
The price in lives was high.

All of us, we will remember
of the original two thousand men,
one-eighty left by mid-September.
A lot of Mothers cried back then.

Some might break down when Buddies die,
most will just have dull stare.
To much death will make the eyes
unseeing, flat, dull, no glare.

Mother nature seems to know
when we have seen to much.
Conscious mind will kind of slow
and "hold our mind in trust."

We lost our colours fighting there,
'cause many men were dying.
Not many know, not many care,
but damn it we were trying.

The "Thirty-Fourth" ceased to exist,
our numbers were to few.
.The "Twenty-First" next on my list,
their numbers were down too.

Bed Check Charley in BI-wing plane,
sounded like a wash machine.
Caused a small amount of pain,
Bed Check was brave and mean.

Some nights at sundown from the West,
he'd drop his bombs on what seemed best.
One night at sundown he glided in,
I guess we seemed what's best to him.

Bombs from plane came swishing down,
got all my squad but me.
Caught my men on open ground,
million dollar wounds you see.

They're going home and they're okay,
a long life should be theirs.
Won't have to fight, not one more day,
they're thru with warring cares.

Crossed the Thirty-eighth parallel
in this land of war torn strife.
Near a small town viewed warriors hell,
commies had no regard for life.

POWs with wired hands
behind their backs were tied.
Face down in bloody stinking sand,
murdered is why they died.

A saying at this period in our history was "Better to be dead than red" orated mostly by flag waving politicians who never had to face the truth of their garbage. They never adequately funded the Armed Forces at Infantry Division level (who must fight on the ground) 'til after we were at war, our tactics and training were as lacking as our worn out World War II armaments.

The lines "these Mothers Children, they're not red" express my total disdain for politicians who send young Boys to a war for which they have not been prepared in tactics or arms. The apathetic bastards in the early stages did not even supply us with enough ammunition for our rifles and machine guns. There were no replacement barrels for the machine guns, we wore the rifling out and were left with smooth bores that sent the tracers ripping thru the air like a wounded duck, causing inaccuracy in direct and overhead fire as the result.

It was many years before I realized monetary support for peacetime military was and is a non-priority item for our Congress. A great deal of funding went to the Air Force in research and development, the Grunts on the ground? Just enough for occupation duties, this was a deep betrayal to all Grunts who were/are the most expendable. Not one politician has or ever will answer for these betrayals nor even recognize death can be caused by lack of funding for adequate continous training and armaments.

Again I declare we have executed some percentage of our own under-trained Boys as surely as if we lined them up before a firing squad and Congress gave the order to "FIRE". Some will disagree. One good aspect is our dead will never know of their betrayal nor that the system of government they fought to defend was in fact their nemesis, a motherland that devoured its young.

jimmie joe

Bullet holes in back of heads,
We'd seen this crap before.
these mothers children, they're not red.
God I hate this stinking war.

But on we went to whip a nation,
could do nothing for these men.
Left them for graves registration,
a quick prayer then — amen.

.Civilian dead seem every where,
killed by retreating Commies.
Two or three hundred in one ditch,
Grand-parents, Kids and Mommies.

In dead Mothers arms Babies held close,
killed by the Commie slime.
These visions plagued my mind the most
after I'd left my warring time.

Even after all these years
of pushing back the "Ghosts."
Most times are fine and not yet tears,
visions of Children hurt the most.

Many "Ghosts" flit thru my head,
can't hide them all the time.
'Cause I'm not dead, nor am I red,
they flit out from warring slime.

I do feel sad 'bout those in ground,
who were little more than Boys.
I do thank God I'm still around
and tasting all life's joys.

The flitting "Ghosts" within my head,
kinda sneak out when guard is down.
I force them back, beats being dead,
it's the only way I've found.

We headed north still going fast
our war was nearly won.
Had the commies whipped at last,
previous months have not been fun.

.Should be soon I'll cross the sea
and hold this love who stole my heart.
My first love Helen waits for me
and our life together we will start.

Arms, warm arms and much, much more,
I have missed my Helen so.
Generals said we're home by Christmas.
A happy Soldier jimmie joe.

Some thanked God upon their knees,
in fairness that seemed just.
God answered with the Red Chinese,
who is this God we trust?

Thus began the longest retreat in American military history. Please note this retreat did not take place under the Grunts orders, the Generals and I assume very high politicians were the ones responsible for the ordering a "tactical withdrawal". Our supply lines were far to long to take on the Chinese Army, we in many cases had to fight our way thru encirclement to even make a retreat. Supplies become critical quite quickly under those circumstances.

Without a withdrawal we would have been wiped out with losses in the tens, possibly hundreds of thousands. There wasn't a chance of ammo and all the supplies needed would reach us in time or in continued abundance we would need against such numbers. Some Divisions held as ordered while other divisions moved thru to the south as ordered, some suffered heavy casualties in this holding so others could escape. The Second Infantry Division was one of the holding divisions and took heavy casualties.

Half a million more or less,
of Chinese "volunteers"?
Again we're in an awful mess,
more Mothers shed more tears.

Bugles, whistles in the night,
this is not a pleasant place.
Guess we'll have a fire fight,
there's egg on Mac Arthur's' face.

Artillery pounding, light by flares,
cordite fumes abound.
Sure is an eerie night out there,
hot shrapnel slices 'round.

Tracers streaking 'cross the sky,
machine-gun barrel glows near red.
wave on wave they come; They die.
Can't believe unnumbered dead.

Our ammunition's getting low,
can't hold out too long.
Soon, real soon we'll have to go
or death will end life's song.

Chinese withdraw, regroup a bit,
gave us respite from this fight.
"Politicians full of shit"!
I'm sure I said that right.

They kissed their god (Mac Arthur's ass),
your "Hero" from the "Big" war.
Politicians caused what's come to pass,
what are we dying for?

Politicians could have ceased
the war by mid-November.
Instead the damn thing just increased,
in sad anger I'll remember.

While politicians pissed themselves
Mac Arthur had his way.
A half a million Red Chinese?
We'll just scare them all away.

We must have scared them to distraction,
perhaps we were a fool.
We scared them in the wrong direction,
south to south of Seoul.

That's the trouble with Infantry
when politicians do not try.
We're the ones who have to cope,
we're the ones who die.

They cut us off last of November,
do not know the date.
Kind of hazy, can't remember
don't like these hands of fate.

I know we had a huge air drop,
the waves flew three abreast.
Cargo drop on old rice crop,
those Pilots were the best.

Wave on wave as they flew past,
c-119s tipped up their nose.
They dropped us what we need at last,
There were no winter clothes.

Ammo, hand grenades and food,
our outlook was improving.
Sure put us in a hopeful mood,
once more we'll get a moving.

Gasoline for trucks and tanks,
mortar rounds and we gave thanks
for cargo drops from overhead.
Now most of us won't end up dead.

Turkeys here for us the living,
most were not quite done.
They dropped us some for our thanksgiving,
we ate them every one.

Ice-cream (melted), can't believe
we would get this now.
Surely eyes of mine deceive,
a last meal? Holy cow!

We made it out to safer ground,
there's not much more to tell.
Chinese no more us do surround
but it's getting cold as hell.

Christmas Eve, cold full moon night,
Artillery lobbed no harassing rounds.
Twenty-four hour truce from fight,
we had peace but cold abounds.

That was the most beautiful Christmas Eve I have in my memory. The full moon reflected light so bright the sky seemed to have a dark blue hue. Small, white puff clouds drifted lazily past the moon and across the dark blue sky. It was deadly cold, deadly silent and absolutely beautiful when combined with the twenty-four hour truce from battle. The guns all along the front were silent, without even the distant sound of harassing artillery fire.

It would be nearly fifty years before a full moon and Christmas Eve would next be wedded in the heavens. I would be an old man remembering the peace a Boy had felt when the sounds of battle had ceased and the moon shone full and bright. It was a grand Christmas Eve, carried in my head for some reason as a special beauty thru time.

Carols streamed 'cross no mans land,
'twas beautiful to hear.
Ladies voices, big brass bands,
hadn't heard them in a year.

Tonight my Helen I really miss,
how I long for her embrace.
To hold her close, to share a kiss.
To touch my Helen's face.

Chinese speakers to make us sad,
guess they were not too bright.
They screwed up, it made us glad,
took us home for just one night.

We crossed the Han in dead of night,
the bridge was later blown.
Formed our lines dug in to fight,
I'm cold wish I was home.

We heard the blowing of the bridge across the Han River from a distance. While researching the Korean War I learned in nineteen ninety-eight the bridge had been filled with refugees and stragglers from South Korean military when the charges were touched off. If this was done accidentally or intentionally I don't know. They would have blown it intentionally while loaded with innocent Humans had they thought the Chinese might save the bridge. I would not have believed this at the time, there is no question in my mind now.

It seems we could have defended the approaches to the bridge until all the refugees had crossed then blow it when the Chinese were on it. At this late date I find there was, in far too many cases, too much disregard for the helpless confused refugees caught and killed in the turmoil of a war not of their making. Where is the glory?

There is much an Infantryman does see in war, there is much more garbage taking place far beyond the foxholes we never know about. It's only years later we may discover the true extent of horrors in "our just cause", the true extent of all politicians involved in the politics of war.

We held our lines against our foe,
can't remember firefights?
.How we did it I don't know
but we must have done it right.

Damn it was cold, In can't believe,
twenty some below I'm told.
The clothes we had could not relieve
that penetrating cold.

Fingers and feet were always numb
and frostbite did abound.
It was a bit unpleasant place,
that cold Korean ground.

A fox hole in the winter time
can freeze one's hands or feet.
It's not a place I'd call sublime.
Why do I think Alaska's neat?

Spring offensive time to go,
frozen fox holes are behind.
Still two feet of melting snow,
it's warm now so that's fine.

On we went again toward north
fighting the Chinese Reds.
The whole UN all blasted forth
this time we have less dead.

The first time in almost a year
we left the forward lines.
Division went division rear,
that peace was really fine.

Our Flag flew there beside a tent,
it stood out in the breeze.
.I finally felt what My Flag meant,
My Flag my heart did please.

Forget what politicians say,
for reelection it's a spin.
Our homeland it is far away,
far from us fighting men.

Our Buddies dug in left and right,
those who danger with us share.
Are reasons why we stay and fight,
are reasons why we care.

I Don't know why my Flag did cause
My throat to lump, my heart to pause.
I really do not care a wit
for politicians full of shit.

My first loves letters they were fine
they helped me thru the warring time.
They came for seven months or so,
thru summers heat and winters snow.

The last one came in early spring,
the sky was clear and blue that day.
Black was edged around the thing,
My heart, my soul, my world turned gray.

It was the worse time of my life,
I just couldn't understand.
My soul torn out by pen's dull knife.
Alone now in this warring land.

My darling Jim's how it began,
I left it; Went to no mans land.
Sat out there 'twixt foe and friend,
wanting hurt, the hurt to end.

Hand on gun and head on knee,
war and killing so long around,
My Buddies came and rescued me
as I thought peace is in the ground.

I thank them now, I didn't then,
deep despair within me swelled.
Just wanted hurt, the hurt to end.

jimmie joe
fishhook junction, alaska

My Helen

After you've read shadow ghosts
some facts that you should know,
by far my Helen helped the most
for about ten months or so.

The war was not a pleasant place
there's no way it could be,
but I could see my Helen's face,
her letters did soothe me.

My mind would leave this place of war
and journey far away,
to a young woman I adore,
to the times when we would play.

The holding hands, the walks in rain,
the closeness we did share,
to everyone it should be plain,
I needed Helen's care.

Thank you Helen for the small piece of time we shared. The pain of that "Dear Jim" letter was quite deep; under combat conditions there was neither room nor time for the grieving. My writings of "my Helen" triggered the release of grief forty-six years later; I also grieved my Helens death twelve years after the fact.

We didn't whip the Red Chinese
did push them back to north.
We didn't do it all alone,
the whole UN sallied forth.

Politicians say we can't wage war
north of the Yalu River.
As China's population soars
this war could last forever.

To those who say we didn't win,
every Harry, Dick or Tom,
did you suggest invade China?
Maybe use the "Atom Bomb"?

You dishonor us who fight for you
when total victory's all you crave.
You dishonor us the living.
You dishonor us in graves.

It's a bit troubling to me the way most of the American public considers we didn't win in Korea. We did win in the sense of freeing South Korea from the North Korean invaders, which in the beginning was the goal. We had them pushed back across the Thirty-eighth Parallel in October, Nineteen-fifty, we had fulfilled the United Nations mandate in a little over three months.

The decision, by Truman, Mac Arthur and God knows who else to reunite the entire Korean Peninsula by force of arms was the triggering mechanism that caused China's becoming engaged. China was paranoid about a world power charging toward her border long before we reached the Yalu River. Flush with her victory over the Chiang Kai-Sheck army only a year earlier she may have also felt the need to puff up the dragon to a size the world would notice. She did exactly that.

The cost in American lives in winning an all out war with China could have been a few hundred thousand. The costs in innocent lives of Chinese Civilians could have been in the tens of millions, possibly hundreds of millions as we incinerated their cities with thermonuclear bombs. Quite disturbing is, there were at the time and still are, a number of Americans, from Mac Arthur down to some average Joe's, who believe total victory is/would be worth the costs in other peoples lives. In my mind only people in the last stages of a degenerative brain disease would trade the "standoff" we accepted with China for a total victory at such a price in Human suffering. Victory is and should remain the objective of armies; total victory at any costs is and should remain in the arena of despots of Hitler's' ilk. There should always be room for a diplomatic end to a war.

"Old Harry" and others were wrong in supporting the push to the Chinese border to achieve the re-unification of the two Koreas. Eisenhower was correct in striving for and accepting the much-delayed process of peace via a stalemate and because of this the Korean War Warriors historically have been seen by many Americans as not quite up to snuff, just didn't meet the Warrior status of their World War II brothers.

Page, 147

> A bullet killed us just as dead,
> hot jagged flying shrapnel too.
> We still held dying Buddies
> as you did in World War Two.

I would ask you to keep in mind the Grunts didn't have anything to say about the political policies of international problems or anything to say about their solutions. The conduct of wars is political processes of both parties and will remain such. The solutions are a political processes by both parties and will also remain such. In a war where one party demands unconditional surrender, such as World War II, the solution is still a political process, albeit a bit one-sided. I ask all politicians to take your bow; you've accomplished much thru my lifetime with the tens upon tens of millions of innocents you've killed in the name of God and Country.

The Grunts returned some with broken bodies, some with broken minds and some with both. Win, lose or draw our country should have cheered their homecoming, acknowledge their sacrifice.

Page 62

> We were hero's back on V- J day.
> The Country partied 'bout a year
> White Crosses still meant nothing.
> I saw no death and felt no fear.

The Grunts from the Korean War returned to a silence we 'most could hear and we kept hearing it for decades. The Grunts from Vietnam returned to a vicious, thankless Goddamn nation, they weren't ignored in silence as the Korean Grunts were, they will remember being cursed and treated with disdain. Even tho not all treated them such, their remembrances of events surrounding their return are seared in their memory banks. Many could not cope with the war they carried in their heads plus the war we gave them here in the States.

So far well over two hundred thousand Vietnam Vets have died by their own hand, but we, their Country's peoples, were the ones who squeezed the trigger. Over five times as many Vietnam Vets have committed suicide as died in the actual war. Can you ask yourselves WHY America? Do you have an answer? No, I don't believe most Americans have ever thought about WHY or questioned the need of an answer. Some still need your answer but their time is running out.

Page, 124

> We fought and died for you America
> and your Warriors you will curse?
> Our Buddies dying hurt quite deep
> but your attitude hurts worse.

Until recently the Department of Veterans Affairs, i.e. the V. A. hospitals have had no real agenda for analyzing and treating of wounds other than physical. The root causes of wounded minds were not treated; the Veterans were guinea pigs for the new experimental drugs. Drugs that managed to mask the problem not cure it, and in the process they managed to fry the brain, not heal it. The wisdom in the treatment of our Vets lacked caring. The caring in the treatment of our Vets lacked wisdom.

Page, 153

Next we visit the VA hospital
for help to ease the pain.
To the physic ward we stay a while
and the Bastards fry our brain.

****

The many wounded nurses serve
in any warring land,
takes courage and a special nerve,
I salute them they are grand.

Day after day I could not do
or face their awful chore,
what Mercy Angles must go thru
to heal Boys wounds of war.

They comfort all us Warriors there,
to us they are divine.
I thank them for the way they care
for us at dying time.

I know that some will later dream
of certain young boys dying.
I pray someone will hold them close,
give them comfort from their crying.

Ship takes me home across the sea,
I hope my Buddies follow me.
Some will die but most should live,
for leaving them please God forgive.

I had a Wife and that was fine,
my Children numbered right at nine.
Most my Grandkids make me smile,
I've caught those fish in places wild.

I've had a real good life you see
Since I sailed home from 'cross the sea.
But thru that life 'most every day
the "Shadow Ghosts" come out to play.

They flit around. They hurt a bit,
and "politicians full of shit."

jimmie joe, fishhook junction, alaska

"Ticking Clocks"

"Ticking Clocks" is not pleasant nor is it intended to be. It is quite candid about the years after ground battles ended and mind battles began. The mind battles caused by the ground battles were the more difficult of the two as they lasted nearly a lifetime.

I thought only I had visions in my head and thoughts flashing in and out thru the years, thoughts hidden from the world until now. I would be constantly pushing them back and arranging them inside walls, building, patching and rebuilding. I felt a bit of shame with my perceived weakness and a bit of fear of ending up in a VA mental ward. In those times, for a military man or Veteran, a section eight was equated with the same fear we had for death or cowardice on the battlegrounds.

I never thought to examine the period of time which forced me to build walls, to try and consciously recall certain memories of combat was a constant struggle to avoid, I was ignorant of therapy or any need of it. I was quite alone with this aspect of my life.

With use of the Internet in 1998, I found many Combat Brothers still carried pain. I wasn't alone. I thank those who responded to my poems. Except via the Internet I never knowingly met a combat Infantryman from the Korean War, the forgotten war really was or tried to be. Men who fought in Korea didn't talk about their war; it took the fiftieth anniversary for our country to recognize our vicious Korean War and the deaths of over fifty-four thousand American Boys. Half a million South Korean troops, over a million Chinese and North Korean's soldiers and several million Korean civilians died. The pain from these losses affect tens of millions for their lifetime and our Troops who survived carry pain filled visions home.

"Ticking Clocks" is for all Veterans of combat; others who read the words may yawn and set it aside. Some, who have been there, will read it, understand and put it on their bookshelf. A few may cry and not put it down until they have absorbed it, I will not be the cause of their tears. Like mine, their tears will be from a young Boy who disappeared on some distant battleground, the Boy who would not accept the unacceptable reality of war, the innocent Boy of our youth who bugged out on us in bloody battle. We miss him. We search for him. We need him home.

From—I never knew him as a Man

> 'Bout then in nighttime battle
> or it could have been in day,
> Boy just kind of up and disappeared.
> He became a different kind of M.I.A.
>
> I think I tried to find him later on,
> maybe for a year or two.
> I don't know how or why he disappeared.
> Guess Boy and I were thru.

When the last of my Children left home the house became an empty lonely place, when I retired from my working years the house was doubly lonely. I could cope with my Ghosts while raising Children; I could cope with my Ghosts while working. I could not ignore or cope with my Ghosts in being alone. In my ignorance there was much I didn't know about the phase of my life that would be played out in the next few years.

1986-1989

My formerly peaceful cabin on the banks of the Little Susitna River became a place I dreaded coming home to each night after the Fishhook Bar closed. I bumbled along for about four years in a steadily more confusing state of limbo, never realizing the deadly course the fates had chosen. I didn't know there was a nineteen-year old Soldier Boy hidden back beyond my brain. A Boy who never left the dying field of a distant battleground, nor that one autumn night in nineteen eighty-nine I would come within a whisker of being a casualty, by my own hand, of a war nearly forty-year-old.

I don't know why my ability to cope left my control; I can't even pin down quite when. I'm probably a classic case of something but damn if I know what. The important point is I made it thru this distressing and dangerous period of my life. Below is my version of this battle, my buildup to the final facing of the fates.

106

My poem "Little Children ———— Grown-ups War", typed by me, written by a nineteen-year-old Boy, was thankfully the healing culmination of Boys time in self-induced purgatory.

jimmie joe

"Ticking Clocks"

I rhymed in Reality and Wanderings
my release of anger and pains of war.
I can not express my reasons
for suppressing warring season.

My memories are not repressed
'cept a few times I can't recall.
It's emotions I would not express,
from Childhood little Boys were told;
Real Men do not bawl.

I don't know if those who read them
will care or understand.
I know I must write all this down,
the years after my killing land.

If I don't express my thoughts to well
as you peruse my rhymes,
please believe I tried like hell.
Can you read between the lines?

In Wandering adjusting of Combat Vets
is mentioned frequently.
These odes cover suppressed ghostly flits
my mind refused to free.

As emotions flowed out from my mind
on paper white with pain in black,
my strong built walls back there in hiding,
my walls of war began to crack.

My walls took over forty years in building,
the patch work was like stone.
It took eighteen months of painful typing
'fore part of me from war came home.

It took 'til old age, all those years,
for me to get things right.
Now old Man cries a young Boys tears.
He'll cry alone, adjust, atone
as he frees subconscious from its night.

Back during times of warring days
conscious mind takes a sabbatical.
Death almost becomes a normal way,
'til our ticking clock we battle.

The battle went on within my mind
after the warring land.
The battles end, no peace I find.
I couldn't try to understand.

They take a lad of just nineteen
and send him off to war.
His mind of pain and death is clean,
it will change forevermore.

Dead buddies locked inside his head,
dead and crippled children too.
Massacred civilians all long dead
but the visions stay quite new.

Throughout time flitting ghosts will roam,
it's tough to keep them in.
Clean nineteen when he left home
to join our fighting men.

Clean nineteen no more is he
but few will understand.
They'll say he went away a boy,
look now and see our Warrior man.

They're so proud to see him standing there,
gosh Dad, he looks so brave and strong.
They can't see inside his crew cut head,
just ticking clock knows something's wrong.

He'll probably live his life all right,
with visions stored in back of mind.
There will be war dreams in the night,
they'll end given some time.

His dreams began in fifty-four,
ghostly death stalked him in sleep.
For several years he'll dream of war.
Societies code inscribed in stone.
Manly men don't weep.

He'll awake sitting bolt upright
as lips close on fading scream.
He ends another nighttime battle.
It's nothing Hon, it's just a dream.

His little Child sleeps in his arms
and makes his heart just glow.
His ticking clock ticks out the harm
and sights of Children long ago.

The long dead Buddies who gave their life,
even the young enemies that died,
they'll not hold a Wife, nor have a Child,
nor catch those Fish in places wild.

I mention this a lot in rhymes,
his visions from long ago.
Unforgiving Ghosts from warring times
drift out from cracks in walls you know.

He'll get real good at hiding pain
but the years after his kids are grown,
fates clock keeps ticking in his brain.
Ticks faster if he's all alone.

He retired from his working years
and his Children left his house.
His time drew near to fight his Ghosts.
'Twill be an unknown mental joust.

He knew nothing of this at the time,
did not know what lay ahead.
It will take a few confusing years
to face his predatory dead.

He may not have been a drinking man
with his Children in his care,
now Ghosts bounce off echoing walls
as clock ticks down to face them square.

It'll take about four years or so,
clock ticks slowly at the first.
He'll begin frequenting the Fishhook Bar
and the cause will not be thirst.

This friendly bar where Ghosts won't roam
kind of soothed his besieged life.
This friendly bar became his home
and somehow smoothed his strife.

.He'll learn to play pool games quite well,
as slowly he drinks more.
While wannabe's brag of their hell
he keeps his own in store.

He didn't tell his war stories,
no heroic deeds he'd done.
He'll play pool, drink and listen to
other Mothers drunken Sons.

Twelve hours a day in bar he'll drink,
He doesn't think about the why.
As clock ticks down toward fates brink
some part inside him grieves to die.
He not yet knows it's time to cry.

He'll head home at closing time
to walls that echo grief.
It'll take a few years more before he knows
ticking clock in bar won't bring relief.

Sleeping will become a real tough chore
as protecting walls begin to crack.
He's filled with hopelessness and more,
forty years his ticking clock turned back.

No Children's laughter, no joy rings out,
no loving mate to hold,
he's sort of lost what life's about,
the Pipers pain will now unfold.

He'd tried the booze it didn't work,
I think he knew it from the first.
His ticking clock caught up one night
as his confused mind caved in.
Ticked time had come to end his fight.
Is old warriors suicide a sin?

His forty-one mag he took to bed,
silently told his friends good-bye.
Cocked it and pressed it to his head
about an inch behind right eye.

His ticking clock was speeding now,
time was nearly at an end.
A bit more pressure on the trigger
and I will lose my lifelong friend.

His Children appeared inside his head
back when they were young.
What are you doing part of brain said,
put down your killing gun.

Pressure on trigger slowly increased,
no thoughts of Heaven nor of Hell.
His ticking clock wants deaths release
for reasons only God can tell.

Your Children and your friends will hurt
if you do this deed,
You've never picked the cowards way,
please Dad your love we need.

He didn't know how long it took,
this argument for escaping or for livin.
For livin trigger pressure relaxed,
for escaping pressure was givin.

His clock would pause then pick up speed
and the seer was he knew not where.
.To cry or die? His unknown need,
the seer didn't really care.

Visions burst from the old Warriors head
that he'd fought to hide thru time.
Those Furies nearly made him dead,
now ticking clock caught warring slime.

He sees despair in men's eyes there,
just before they cloud.
Deaths wounds exposed he sees deaths throes
as men take on deaths shroud.

Children with missing arms or legs
caused by death bombs from the sky.
Orphaned Children with no Mommies.
Starving Children;……….. Children die.

He feels the fear of yesteryear
as men charged 'cross no-mans land.
Sees blood that pumps from legless stumps
as life's force spurts out in sand.

Four haunting eyes locked and staring,
now accusing with their pain.
Will he still feel their accusation
after death relieves his brain?

Will they still appear when he is dead?
Those eyes from long ago.
Eternally harbored in his head?
God, please God don't let it be.
Please don't let that be so.

He sees eyes burned out, hears screaming shouts
as white phosphorus burns men blind.
He feels the pain, sees the insane
as brave men escape their minds.

He sees his Children home at play,
hears their laughter, feels their joy.
Now he's holding little bloodied hands.
Holds mangled Dying Children
locked in time with Soldier Boy.

Now visions raced and visions stopped,
Blurred visions raced once more.
Reality fought time and space.
Pushed back the tearless visions.
Stored his tearless Ghosts of war.

He thought of who would find him dead,
his Daughters or a friend.
Pressure on trigger he slacked off,
can't let them see this kind of end.

Then slowly pistol left his head,
the living won despite his grief.
Those he loves beat warring dead
as his soul cried out for some relief.

Damn it God won't you help me,
I don't want to die alone.
I am lost in pains direction.
The road is long, please God, please help.

The demon fates had nearly taken him
to that land beyond the sky.
His Angel touched him just in time:
jimmie Joe, **Hey!** *jimmie Joe.*
Come on Boy it's time to cry.

For forty years he'd hid deaths tears
from Kin and all he knew.
For forty years he'd hid deaths tears
and from himself he hid them too.

115

He didn't know the why of tears.
Confusion reigned supreme.
Now he felt Boys long hidden pain.
Mans flitting visions; Warring dreams.

Tears gushed from the old Warriors eyes
but they were not old Warriors tears.
The tears were from a Soldier Boy
who's age was nineteen years.

Tears from that far and distant past.
Young tears from eyes of old.
The Pipers being pain at last.
Thru soundless tears past times unfold.

Tears flowed for little Children
with their eyes clouded from pain.
Tears flowed for their senseless dying.
Tears stored back beyond his brain.

Tears flowed for little children's hands
which he'd held so long ago.
Tears flowed out his mournful sorrow
mixed with tears he didn't know.

Tears of guilt flowed for the leaving.
Dying Children tears did mourn.
Questioned, never understanding.
Questioned God, why were they born?

Question why the dying Buddies
in that Land of Morning Calm.
Question reasons for their dying.
Only tears, no soothing balm.

His Daughter found him the next day
huddled and sobbing in his chair.
Ask no questions, just held her dad,
she helped a lot, his times were bad.

I recall only one of my thoughts that night, the rest were too scrambled. The one thought I will not forget as I squeezed the trigger were the words I kept saying over and over as I applied pressure; A little more won't hurt …….. A little more won't hurt……… A little more won't hurt. ……………won't hurt. ……………….. hurt…
I figured it out years later, I'm a bit slow sometimes.
I know my thoughts were bits and pieces of my later rhymes, involved with, a time of conscious need without subconscious release. A time to………. bring back the Boy.

.'Twas along the bloody Naktong River
that I noticed my Chum change.
His eyes lost all their laughing sparkle
and his smile was not the same.

I'll not know what he might have been,
he would not be shaped by warring time.
His walls absorbed the shaping,
and that boyhood friend of mine.

The Boy who left for war is gone.
He was never seen again.
Only I came home from battles.
Now a stranger 'mongst old friends.

One Boy died and one survived
in those days so long ago.
Jim made it into Manhood.
Jim misses jimmy joe.

I hope I get to meet them
in that land beyond the sky.
I'd like to see my Dog "old Gent"
and that Boy who choose to die.

I gained very little therapeutic help from that distraught night; I did gain enough to save me. I unknowingly gained the knowledge of there being a way out, of some nearly fatal flaw I must come to terms with. My Angel had given me a reprieve and the time I would need to find my way, it would be nine years before I found the route leading home, my thoughts continued staying hidden from family and friends. They are now recorded for all to see. Putting pain on paper forced me to examine and squarely face my demons as I read and reread my printed words until no tears were left.

Eisenhower's Papers which I read in Nineteen ninety-seven demanded a response. With sadness, disappointment and anger it's spread throughout my poems. History is so different when viewed with knowledge and time.

True adjusting began as I attempted my response to the treasonous acts of our leaders. The abandonment of our POWs were America's sacrificial victims of political expediency in a War which, after November 1950, we had neither a plan nor any intention of winning. A War best forgotten? It was... by most that weren't involved in it, or lose a Son, or having been there as one of the Korean peoples.

The final poem "Little Children—Grown-ups War" was my road leading home, a forty-seven year saga along a twisting, sometimes straight, smooth, sometimes-bumpy road. I'd have found my way sooner but I was never given a road map and the journey was thru lands I had never traversed. My vision sometimes became quite blurred, all making the journey more difficult and time consuming. The first few years were mostly dead ends; my road was a rat's maze. As I bounced off many roadblocks I slowly learned to put up walls of directions so I would not take those turns again.

When I had built enough walls I was able to feel my way along and my road smoothed out for many years with only unexpected potholes. I would work around them and continue on, remembering their locations and ministering the blisters of my soul.

Near roads end all the potholes from my journey combined to form one huge hole with no way around, I was forced to fill it in with Boys precious protective walls. As I tore the walls down Kim and Leaha's tears began to flow from my eyes, four little helping hands appeared to assist me in the filling, two small Korean Children paved it with Forgiveness, understanding and yes, I felt and still feel their Love. My imagination? My heart says no. Thank you Kim and Leaha, daddy loves you too.

My saga has ended and I shall not pass that way again.

jimmie joe

(Winter of 1999/2000). Hello jimmie joe it's been a long time, lets head to the southern Ozarks for the winter. We'll catch some bluegills and spend a lot of wasted time just wasting time

> Took a few years but worked out fine.
> He can see it as he reads my rhymes.

I am very thankful my friend didn't end his life in Nineteen eighty-nine and I thank the Lord for what ever saved him. A lot of Vets don't make it past their crisis point. —Sadly, their life ends in despair.

I am quite ashamed I never considered or thought about the series of events, that in an instant of time with no one interceding would cause a Brother to end his life. I now realize demons can lurk for years, keeping the Boy away and patiently waiting, waiting for that one instant, his time of despondency and confusion, to kill him in a war that is thirty, forty or fifty years old. —— I know it happens. —I do not know why.

The way out can not be that instant in time, only an Angel, luck or whatever you care to call it will save you then. The way out is to realize that instant in time will, does or can exist, believe me it can. Get help long before you reach this stage, otherwise you may cause family and friends pain you have no right to put them thru.

Again I say putting my pain on paper, where I was forced to face it, was for me very healing. I pray "Ticking Clocks" will help some Brothers before they face their instant in time. Please know you are not alone. I'm not a shrink; my story is the best I can do. May God bless and guide you.

A lot of Vets have died by their own hand,
none really know the reason why.
Damn clocks ticked down from killing land.
We just tell our friend good-bye.
We're sorry Buddy

jimmie joe,
fishhook junction, alaska

My journey to my view of responsible citizenship

I took sixty-two years to learn the correct spelling of Republican; I needed to go from being raised a Democrat (forty years), thru "the hell with it" stage (ten years), and thru the independent stage (twelve years). I finally learned damnrepublican was not one word and Republicans are not all rich, some are almost like you and me except of course they are quite a bit uglier.

There will be those who will take umbrage with some of my writings, ultra-conservatives or ultra-liberals may agree or disagree, they can write me off as a whiner or a warmonger I could care less, nearly anything with ultra preceding it I don't seem to care for.

The liberals are that which I fear most, thru their policies my Children, Grandchildren and Great Grand-children, each generation has known less and less freedom. To each generation their moment in time is the status quo, they'll never know that which has been taken from them. What I see as intrusion on Freedoms they will see and accept as normal.

The Liberals have been the ones in power, in both houses of Congress and the Executive Branch, each time we went to war in the twentieth century, minus of course Desert Storm

I was born a Democrat, my parents, grandparents and every relative I've ever known has been a democrat. I actively campaigned in Alaska for President Johnson against Barry Goldwater in 1964 and was proud when Johnson won the election. I was afraid Goldwater would get us into a war. I never dreamed what Johnson would turn Vietnam into with his Gulf of Tonkin lie.

I also never dreamed the Johnson administration would set the wheels in motion for the subjugation of my Alaska. The appointment of Stewart Udall in the mid-sixties as secretary of the Interior would begin the environmental and liberal lobby, which would eventually run the war, yes to some of us it is a war, a war to shape my Alaska into an image projected by themselves, for themselves. The promises in our statehood compact of nineteen fifty-nine have been rendered null and void over the last thirty-five years, the equal treatment clause of our constitution has not been met as it applies to my Alaska. Liberals have made my Alaska much less free and caused great mental anguish to us, Alaska's Children.

The official Alaska Flag Song

Eight stars of gold on a field of blue,
Alaska's flag, may it mean to you,
The blue of the sea, the evening sky.
The mountain lakes and the flowers nearby.
The gold of the early sourdough's dream,
The precious gold of the hills and streams,
The brilliant stars in the northern sky,
The Bear, the Dipper, and shining high,
The Great North Star with it's steady light,
O'er land and sea, a beacon bright.
Alaska's Flag. to Alaskan's dear,
The simple flag of a Last Frontier.

With the huge build up of ground troops due to the Gulf of Tonkin lie, the general vast escalation of the war in Vietnam, and the cover-up of My Lai I finally had to much of liberalism and its' lies. My Lai caused great turmoil in my soul, it cast a pall on the honour I personally felt about our government. I live by my code of Honour and I expected my government's code to be no less. With knowledge from time and history I have been forced to conclude our governments code of conduct is flawed.

I was ignorant of many aspects of my governments conduct in domestic and foreign affairs, I was especially ignorant of our leaders looking the other way when atrocities were committed by the South Korean Army in Korea. Our government knew about the atrocities and did not stop them, I find that dishonourable.

My expectations of our politicians honour was I not met in Korea, Vietnam, Panama and Clinton's Afghanistan, Sudan, Serbia and Kosovo. Honour has left us thru the death of innocents who had nothing to do with what the executive branch perceives as it's God given right. The right to use our armaments; Bombs, rockets and cruise missiles on innocent peoples trapped in the wars we were actively engaged in or later as a lesson to terrorists.

Abducting a leader of a sovereign nation for his part in the drug trade or, worse than the others, as a distraction for the press and the public from what was taking place in the executive branch. We kill innocents in all cases, it is sad I've lost the belief in America I once carried so proudly.

I am totally appalled by the lack of honour on our domestic front in the years 1993 thru 2000, all the liberal excuses and lies to justify Clintons very existence as the perjuring head of liberal liars.

We have become bullying aggressors by that which we do without "just cause". We have become, in many cases our own enemy, an enemy of the freedoms men have died to preserve. The use of bombs or missiles launched against another country is an act of war, no if, ands or buts. Being a world power does not give us honour, does not give us special rights we have presumed to take. Congress has given it's funding and therefore it's approval to acts of war against nations that have been no threat to America, weak nations with no recourse. Innocents dying by our hands seems to upset very few of us, we've lost our Homeland.

All I had seen as an adult in the running of our country by the liberals were questionable wars in which several million civilians were killed and over one-hundred thousand of Americas young became a bit of clay in flag draped coffins.

The war on poverty's a joke, a damn expensive joke I might add, we've trapped the past generations into the dependence on and total need of taxpayer largesse, Liberals have kept them as children. Liberals have kept them as voters. I was worried about Goldwater being president? I worried too much, I was wrong again.

We were unprepared for World War II even tho it was well known we would be at war with Japan and Germany. Well known by Roosevelt and the higher echelons of government whose only plan of preparation was hiding the American public's head in the sand so as not to get them upset prematurely. The military basically remained under-funded, under-trained, under-prepared and the top peoples, especially Roosevelt knew war was coming, we were set up.

They knew that by being so unprepared some of our young Boys in the military would be sacrificed and they knew it would take that sacrifice to bring America fighting mad into World WAR II. *They were correct.* Enlistment offices were mobbed on Dec. 8, 1941.

Our young Boys paid the price at Pearl Harbor and worse yet in the Philippines, those Boys died defending the Philippines without adequate armament, ordnance, training or a chance in hell of winning. A little over half survived the Bataan Death March, the ship transports and the Prisoner of War camps to return home nearly four years later.

The Bataan Death March, was a forced march of 70,000 (About 12,000 were American) and Filipino prisoners of war captured by the Japanese in the Philippines. <"

HYPERLINK "< http://www.neta.com/~1stbooks/bataan1.htm >"

On Dec. 7, 1941, Japan attacked Pearl Harbor. The American Pacific Naval Fleet suffered heavy losses in lives and ships. The Fleet was incapacitated and could not, in that state, defend American interest in the Pacific Rim and in Asia. Only eight hours later on Dec. 8, 1941 Japan launched an aerial attack on Philippines.

Most of the American Air Force in the Philippines was destroyed while the planes were on the ground. **Eight hours after Pearl Harbor our planes were caught on the ground**? A few days' later, Japanese forces landed on the Philippines. The Japanese landings were in Northern Luzon and in the Southern Mindanao Islands. Inexperienced troops failed to stop the Japanese at the landing. Mac Arthur had to revert back to the original plan, withdrawing the Filipino-American forces into the Bataan Peninsula. By the January 2, 1942, the Northern Luzon forces were in-place for the defense of Bataan.

The Filipino-American Defense of Bataan was hampered by many factors: A shortage of food, ammunition, medicine, and attendant materials. Most of the ammunition was old and corroded. The AA shells lacked proper fuses, as did many of the 155mm artillery shells. Tanks, Trucks, and other vehicles were in short supply, as was the gasoline needed to power these items of warfare.

Poorly trained Filipino troops, most of who never fired a weapon, were thrown into frontline combat against highly trained Japanese veterans. Americans from non-combatant outfits: such as air corpsmen and, in some instances, even civilians, were formed into provisional infantry units.

The Defenders of Bataan continued to hold their ground, without reinforcements and without being re-supplied. Disease, malnutrition, fatigue, and a lack of basic supplies took their toll.

On March 11, 1942, Gen. Mac Arthur was ordered to Australia, Gen. Wainwright took his place in Corregidor, as Commander of the Philippine forces and Gen. King took Wainwright's place, as Commander of the Fil-

American forces in Bataan. Around the latter part of March, Gen. King and his staff assessed the fighting capabilities of his forces, in view of an impending major assault planned by Gen. Homma. Gen. King and his staff determined the Fil-American forces, in Bataan, could only fight at 30% of their efficiency, due to malnutrition, disease, a lack of ammunition and basic supplies, and fatigue. On April 3, 1942, the Japanese launched their all out final offensive to take Bataan.

On 9 April 1942, Gen. King surrendered his forces on Bataan, after the Japanese had broken through the Fil-American last main line of resistance. More on Bataan see URLs below.

<

HYPERLINK "http://home.pacbell.net/fbaldie/Outline.html"

HYPERLINK "http://home.pacbell.net/fbaldie/In_Retrospect.html"

We had the lead-time, damn it we had over two years to be well prepared, there was no excuse for the Generals and politician's complacency, and many thousands of Deaths should not have been. These Deaths rest on the backs of politicians and show the disdain liberal politicians hold for our "Little Tin Soldiers" when we are in a small war or at peace. As children they probably played war games with throwaway tin soldiers. They didn't change and their liberal anti-military thought process is the same today.

HYPERLINK "http://home.pacbell.net/fbaldie/In_Retrospect.html"

Less than five years after the end of World War II we were again at war, this time in Korea, a poor, rural, impoverished country about the size of Minnesota, a Civil War so to speak.

The Democrats controlled the House, the Senate and the Executive branch, as you might have guessed we were again unprepared, possibly more so than at the onset of WWII.

Young Boys again died needlessly, we didn't learn. Politicians of mostly Liberal bent had been willing to trade lives of young Boys for smaller defense budgets. They still believe a well trained, well-equipped Military is not needed in peacetime. *They will not/do not learn. Liberals still say today; "we aren't at war, we don't need so much for defense;*

"Hell no one is a threat to us now, or lets use the Military to stop drugs along our border with Mexico." (The most important aspect of an individual Warriors survival will be lost: [Constant disciplined Cohesive Unit Training])

I ask in all sincerity;

"Have you seen Boys panic, run, and die due to the lack of cohesive unit training?"

"Have you seen Boys die due to outdated armament or being untrained to improvise/repair in the field?"

"Have you seen Boys die due to the lack of supplies, or ordnance that would not do the job?"

"Have you seen Boys die due to the lack of well trained, well disciplined Officers and Noncoms?"

"Have you seen Boys die?"

I ask those questions and most Liberals will not connect their answer to my questions, they do not equate: *The reality of death on a battleground to the lack of cohesive unit training, or The Honour of a Rangers Black Beret' to a whole damn army of black berets'.*

The liberals have lowered standards in basic Infantry training so females could compete in a ground combat role. "Hell we can do less training, give 'em all a black beret' and we'll have some fine looking fighting men", Oops I mean persons. Social engineering should not be attempted where the results on a battleground will be unknown, if females desire to become "Amazon Warriors" let it be in an all female battalion or division. The lowering of intensity and difficulty of training will only increase the number of needless deaths when Troops enter combat.

Liberals see our Warriors as charging up a hill with bayonets fixed, they know we aren't quite real people; real people wouldn't do such a damn thing! Thousands died needlessly due to liberals being in power and shortchanging the military thru the past sixty years and if Americans are aware of this they don't give a damn.

Gulf of Tonkin? Politicians even lie to each other to get us killed. Johnson's LIE, this lie would live thru the last ten years of the Vietnam War. A Democratic Congress every year would fund the lie and a Democratic Congress every year would fund the killing. Flower children would be spitting on our returning Warriors; A Democratic Congress would be funding basic training for their newest crop of young American males.

Johnson was totally responsibly for the huge build-up of ground forces and for the criminal tactic of "free fire zones" with a predictable result of a "My Lai". In a war where the enemy wore "black Pajamas" and you never knew who was the enemy it is a tribute to our Troops that there weren't more "My Lai's".

Nixon becoming President in early Nine-sixty-nine and the expanding of the war into Laos, Cambodia and bombing the hell out of North Vietnam does not say much about the Republicans attempt at a peaceful resolution, again winning, right or wrong, was the unquenchable demand of their egos. Losses of life become quite secondary when politician's egos are involved. The same type of damn egos were involved in the last two years of the "Korean Police Action", again we had a Democratic House, a Democratic Senate and Old Harry. In the North we bombed the hell out of the cities for twenty-six additional months. Near the Thirty-Eighth Parallel we would take the same hills and ridges, lose the same hills and ridges, over and over again for twenty-six months as the death toll mounted, a million? Two million added deaths? No one knows. None really cared then or question it now.

We only know for sure more Warriors died, many more innocent Civilians died as their are more of them when the bombs fall on cities, there are more of them to die from disease, from suicide and from starvation. I sincerely doubt if you will find many Soldiers who died of starvation. Soldiers have the guns, they eat first.

Vietnam, 1962 - 1975, a Democratic Congress would not stop the war nor demand the winning of it, just authorize it's continuation, year after year after year after year. Can you get it thru your heads flower children? It was Congress not the Grunts, the Grunts Died. Politicians devoured them and sent the Bones home in Flag draped Coffins to become a mound of earth. Honoured by our government in Death. Disdained by flower children in life.

Flower children burned, pissed on and stomped our flag and by proxy those mounds of earth. Gold Star Mothers knelt and prayed beside those mounds, a bit of wet clay for Mom as a gift from the caring altruistic flower children.

As of 1998 over 200,000 Vietnam Vets had committed suicide and joined their Buddies in those mounds of earth, in part put there by you flower children, your actions of over thirty years ago keeps killing them. We did not have this high rate of suicide following either the Korean War or World War II.

It was Congress damn you Congress, not the Grunts. I believe you knew. I think it was the in thing and you were in. No danger of jail for harassing the Grunts and no guts to take on our politicians.

While you did have a large part in the stopping of the war in Vietnam your methods had a larger part in the death thru suicide of Warriors who fought in the Vietnam War. As Warriors must cope with the memories of war itself, they must also cope with the treatment their country gives them when they arrive back in the States. Their country and their peers for many years betrayed them.

> We fought and died for you America
> and your Warriors you will curse?
> Our Buddies dying hurt quite deep
> but your attitude hurts worse.
>
> Our adjusting we had to face alone,
> there was no counseling long ago.
> A few inside their minds did not come home,
> their minds still hold what you won't know.

For the two hundred thousand plus Vietnam Veterans who have committed suicide the Wall of Honour came either too late or their Ghosts were to demanding. Sadly their names will not appear as "killed in action" even tho in reality many of them were.

The Wall

The Vietnam Memorial is nearly sacred in my mind; it causes sorrow to well up in my heart that is far and above any other memorial, book, movie or any thing I can name in this world. The Vietnam Black Wall of Honour seems to hold an aurora of Spirits that are to me tangible. Those Spirits are there for us, they heal us, be we Vietnam Vets, Korean Vets or any combat Vets. It is a Wondrously unique and therapeutic oasis for the hidden recesses of a pained soul, a soul who has lived the reality of a war zone and survived, survived to discover his war didn't end with his return from battle. We all need an oasis such as the; **"Black Marble Wall"**

My shoes will fit most Grunts, some will pinch and some will walk right out of them. Some will have Ghosts and no shoes, I'll try to lend them mine for a short while, and mine are broken in and without the blisters of nearly fifty years. If some writings hurt and cause tears my Friend there is a need, if not? That's great.

jimmie joe

Young Warrior —— Old Veteran

.I can't remember my rotation
from that bloody killing land.
Can't remember leaving Buddies
and I don't understand.

Subconscious mind will not release
in leaving should I atone?
The living friends I left to fight,
to fight and die alone.

I was not aware these thoughts were there,
must have been repressed back thru time.
While typing thoughts, my soul to bare,
my guilt flowed out in rhyme.

I remember being on a ship
in middle of Pacific.
Euphoria filled my mind with peace,
I felt really terrific.

Safe and going home was I,
I'd survived that killing ground.
I'm going to live, not going to die,
mixed emotions did abound.

That might seem kind of nuts to you
but to me was a revelation.
I was thru with death and war,
I'd survived that bloody warring nation.

I knew I might now have a wife,
could have and hold a child.
Again I'd see my Mom and Dad
and catch those Fish in places wild.

I've made it home the battle's over,
I can't believe it's true.
The stench of death and rice paddies
and dying friends are thru.

As I ride home on plane or train
or on a greyhound bus.
I look around and life is normal,
my war has caused no fuss.

I noticed as I travel
thru this homeland of the free,
there's none that care, they all ignore,
Boys dying 'cross the sea.

.Back then the thought was not disturbing,
at least not in a conscious way.
I now was thru with mankind's war
and my life in peace would be okay.

Friends and family were 'near like strangers,
something was not as it should be.
Home was the same as when I left.
The stranger friend was me.

My world was somehow different
but it wouldn't register for years.
My war would stay way back in hiding.
'Til I released the long stored tears.

I know how odd to some this seems,
my subconscious was locked tight.
Took two more years to start war dreams
and fight alone in dark of night.

'

In the daytime I'd seem normal,
folks will not know all's not well.
Later on in sleep, I'll scream, I'll weep.
My war's now fought in nighttime's hell.

I began to hate the sleep time,
with the same dreams without an end.
Always alone with nighttime battle,
always alone, no Comrade Friend.

They train us well to fight in war,
train us to kill and maybe die.
They don't train us for aftereffects.
What about our time to cry?

.So we go for years always on guard,
that wall must be strong we know.
Caught by surprise with chance remark
and damn tears begin to flow.

We patch the breach quite quickly
and feel embarrassed for our friend.
We make a note inside our heads,
this subject won't come up again.

I thought something was wrong with me,
a weakness I must hide.
The hurting, flitting ghosts I'd see,
I must push back deep inside.

Other combat Vets don't feel this way,
with these damn Ghosts in their head.
The other combat Vets all seem okay,
we never know 'cause nothing's said.

Nothing's said 'cause no one knows,
alone we drift thru years.
'Round and 'round the clocks hand goes,
alone we suppress tears.

For many years the ghosts hide deep
and flit out now and then,
should not take forty years to weep,
even for Warrior men.

Now that I have let them out
thru sometimes painful, tearful rhymes,
Vets who've read my poems know it's about
they're not alone with hurting times.

.The guilt and pain is standard fare
to some Warriors from their war.
The sharing when our souls we bare
might help someone's hidden inner core.

You're not alone in how you feel
with Ghosts of War that roam.
My prayers for you my Friend are real.
At long last I say, Son Welcome Home".

The Shadow Ghosts began to roam
and flit out now and then,
there was no peace in coming home,
my warring dreams began.

You've read about the two small kids
back there in Shadow Ghosts,
Of three or four repeating dreams
by far those hurt the most.

I'd wake from dreams a crying,
at times in them I'd scream.
I'd dream of Buddies dying
or little Children and morphine.

Subconscious mind slipped out at night,
of that I'd no control.
I'm tired of this, this endless fight,
I don't want dreams; please not tonight.

This time of life it held no joy,
for me, his country's Soldier boy.
Outside my head I seemed all right,
some inside part held dark of night.

.I'd dream of things that were not real?
At least I can't recall.
Why could I cope in actual war
and in dreams not cope at all?

The dreams went on, I can't remember,
a couple years I guess.
It was a quite confusing time,
my mind in sleep won't rest.

Those dreams all really scared me,
they scared me thru and thru.
Dear God don't take away my mind,

I don't know what to do. Please God it's up to you.
Later God might have helped me,
a voice in my dreams would say,
"wake up jim, it's just a dream."
I'd awake and be okay.

Dreams came less and less and less,
no more tears or fears; no screams.
After while I was back to
my flying jumping dreams

The visions here within my head,
I know that they will stay.
Was better then to cope with them,
When dreams finally went away.

jimmie joe

War is a deadly serious undertaking, our young Warriors will not realize this in the beginning, they will learn quite suddenly as they see their Buddies fall. The young Boys will have an excuse, all thru our history, the fact of awarding decorations and medals for bravery has been seen as an initiation into Manhood. Valid or not this is what may very well subconsciously tempt many young men to expose themselves to the dangers associated with harms arena.

The draft fulfills a demanded patriotism and I doubt if the above applies, but to the draftees that are sent into harms way and survive the result will be the same. The rites of manhood will have been met, it's a fallacy of course but a fallacy accepted in general by all societies.

Way back in time men were by necessity the protectors of the family group, later they became the protectors of their Clan and later still their Country. I believe thru the ages we've built upon this "ritual of manhood". When countries came into being politicians had a ready made, deeply rooted cause, for gathering the men they would need for armies, need for power, and need for war.

In all our wars since the end of World War II we have been a little unclear about the real threat our enemy actually carried. We were unclear about any danger to our Family, our Clan or our Country, we neither observed nor felt danger, yet it was demanded we join in battle with an enemy half way around the world. We battled an enemy, contrived by politicians, in a war against an enemy who was no threat to us except in the ideologically paranoiac minds of some politicians. I.e. A cold war anxiety attack? Maybe, but our wars caused the death of millions of innocent Humans, and sadly it was an official game of domino effect. A game played by politicians for nearly half a century. ....*jimmie joe*"

"Tears of Rain"

"A MOUND OF EARTH IS NOW's THEIR WORTH?"
1776 —————— THRU TIME

About one million young men have given their oath to defend the constitution of these United States of America; these men I write of are now mounds of earth. They gave their lives upholding this sacred oath, for our country and us who now live, for our freedom, for their honour. Their honour is eternal, ours is being tested and the test will continue as long as we remain a free Country.

Although our Warriors were young men, in my olden mind we were Boys, with much honour and respect I will refer to them as such. I think deeply about the young boys who gave their lives for this country, this long line of young Boys from the revolution to now, one million strong. Most of them never knew our joys, the joy of a loving Wife, the joy of having their little Child hold their finger as they walked together, never knew the joy of being Grandparent, the simple joy of adult life.

They only knew death while preserving our freedoms thru time, our freedoms right down to each individual, to you now alive in America. Each of us, every one, has a million dead young Boys who gave their lives for the freedoms we still enjoy. We have a sacred obligation to not let these freedoms slip away, an obligation to inform the next generation thru our home and schools of these sacred sacrifices made for us.

I become quite angry at my homeland, which I don't know or understand anymore. My feeling of pride in America has nearly disappeared. I can only remember about three names of my foxhole Buddies but I can well remember pride in my country when I was young. I don't remember when it started to leave; I do know there is not much left. It's quite sad that I must fear for my Grandchildren's future in a free society.

My Children have no idea how little intrusion there was by government in my younger days, the present status quo is their reality and accepted as the norm. This slow eroding of freedoms caused by creeping intrusion of our government into many aspects of our lives will slowly evolve to freedoms demise as each generation passes.

Once lost these freedoms will not be given back or regained by politicians. Politicians are at their best when people threaten them the least, are not answerable to the people, and have nearly total control of the people.

Only politicians can remove our freedoms, only the American people can prevent it from becoming reality. At the very least we should teach "Our Constitution and Bill of Rights" in grades four thru twelve. Has anyone ever questioned why educators ignore this document, this blueprint of our freedoms?

Neither our politicians nor the American peoples are above exchanging our freedoms for the perceived safety of our persons. The mess created by Johnson's Great Society has been coming home to roost for thirty-five years. Ask not what you can do for your country; Ask that which your country can do for you is quite anti-JFK; somehow his slogan became quite skewed beginning with President Johnson.

We are obligated to the infirm and truly disabled, those who would be adults have a severe and sacred duty to their own maintenance, the care of their families and the care of the infirm, No more and no less.

"Our Bill of Rights Amendment number ten" has been the one most corrupted by politicians, they are aware it is the one that gives States the Right to, nay demands, holding the power of the federal government in check. All other "Rights" become progressively more vulnerable as the "Tenth Amendment" becomes more degraded. Power over the States (people) is the agenda federal politicians have been slowly building for one hundred and forty years.

States now are basically powerless; their Constitutions, which were accepted by the Feds at statehood, now, mean nothing in the halls of Congress or the U.S. Supreme Court. Statehood compacts have become one-way streets leading to a way of life where one shoe fits all. We have a D.C. dictatorship, an elected dictatorship whose yoke is placed between Amendments one and two.

You will notice I use the plural of freedom in my poems, freedom is not a singular right We will continue to lose freedoms one by one 'til singular could be all we have left.

For our million "Men of Honour" the ultimate sacrifice was required. They were true to their oath.

Mr. President! Honour our Constitution and Bill of Rights.

Article X.; The powers not delegated to the United States by the Constitution, nor prohibited by it to the States, are reserved to the States respectively, or to the people.

> The ones in power slowly devour
> the freedoms for which men died.
> The enemy's not 'cross the seas,
> inside the beltway they abide.

jimmie joe
fishhook junction, Alaska

"Tears of Rain"

There's a price we pay for freedoms
and for some the price was high.
Our long dead Warriors paid this price,
for our freedoms they did die.

Most do not care 'bout their death there,
a half a world away.
Most give no thought to price that bought
the rights we have today.

Some should take heed and do not read
these rhymes in "Tears of Rain."
The graphic speech is meant to teach
freedoms cost in death and pain.

It's rhymed to show the debt we owe
our long dead Warrior men.
Deaths debt unpaid, payments not made,
thru time debt will not end.

We're guardians now, I fear somehow
for our constitutions decree,
as time travels on I feel we're pawns
of feds back in DC.

In congress halls freedoms do pause
their oath of office they have spurned.
An oath's that's made is a debt unpaid,
it's time the bastards learned.

It's up to us, deaths debt of trust,
our constitution to defend.
Freedoms loss is slow and some politicians know
it just takes time my friend.

Each freedom lost dishonour costs
the ones who make the rules.
Honour will drain from despots brains
as we remain their childish fools?

When people choose freedoms to lose
for their own uncaring gain
and freedoms call has left us all,
Warriors deaths will be in vain.

For my country dear I hold great fear
as federal intrusion grows.
Infringement on life is cause for strife,
still we go with status quo.

The ones in power slowly devour
the freedoms for which men died.
The enemy's not 'cross the seas,
inside the beltway they abide.

I am well aware that damn few care
'bout Warriors death in bloody pain.
Memorial Day's a day for play
not for Warriors who were slain.

.Dead Warriors cause should make us pause
and question why they gave their life.
Question why men die as loved ones cry,
question why men faced such strife.

Throughout the years with pain and fears,
young men have gone to die.
Freedom meant more than death in war
and freedoms did survive.

Our freedoms now near lost somehow,
slowly they slipped away.
Like melting snow in spring they go.
Charge us a Judgment Day.

Rise up, rise up our Warriors dead,
your resting days are thru.
Your country needs you once again,
lost honour calls for you.

Thru history our enemy
you defeated back thru time,
You faced wars strife and gave your life
for your loved ones and mine.

In honour you died, to death you tried
and did your job damn well.
But now my friends, my long dead friends
our honour slips toward hell.

Most only know the status quo
of government today.
Of freedoms lost, the ones we've tossed
they comprehend no way.

.There are no fights for lost states rights,
the opposite is a fact.
Our men who fought 'twill be for naught
'til freedoms we earn back.

Did you die in vain? It's with great pain
I call you from your sleep.
Rise up from graves our Warriors brave,
the ones who care now weep.

Your song of life ended in strife
and your spirits drift in sky,
joining those before who died in war,
forming clouds as freedoms die.

As dark clouds form spirits will mourn
freedoms loss and feel more pain,
They'll face once more their death in war
and tears will fall, their Tears of Rain.

Us who now live please do forgive,
we've let freedoms slip asunder.
We need you friends, dead Warrior friends,
unleash your cannons' thunder.

Bring all your dead, make us all dread
we caused your country's' fate.
Show us life's blood, wounds mixed with mud,
show "Freedoms bloody mate."

For freedoms cause you didn't pause,
show the price keep us free.
Show buddies dead, ripped wounds that bled,
show legs blown off at knees.

.Show us the fear of yesteryear
as you charged 'cross no mans land.
Show blood that pumps from legless stumps
as life's' blood spurts out in sand.

Show eyes burned out and screaming shouts
as white phosphorus burns you blind.
Show us the pain, show the insane
as brave men escape their minds.

Show Warriors brave in lonely graves
ten thousand miles from home.
"That mound of earth now's all their worth?"
Preserving freedoms will atone.

None lay a wreath, none cry their grief,
none tend the mournful graves.
Few truly care 'bout their death there.
Forgotten Warriors brave.

Show machine-gun rip from neck to hip
as slugs rake a buddies life.
Above his hair in helmet there,
photo of one to be his wife.

His last act will be to try and see
this picture of his love.
Last words we hear are Jenny dear,
spirit leaves for sky above.

M-1 rifle upside down
fixed bayonet stabbed deep in ground,
helmet placed atop the thing,
one dogtag on chain does swing.

My body's here sweet Mother dear
but my spirit's soared away.
I've left war's hell and I will dwell
with you when we would play.

I'm here with you and Jenny too,
I'm still your little man.
I love you Mom and I'm not gone.
I just come home —— Left warring land.

The veil
A Warriors passing

Mom tell my Dad please don't be sad,
I really am alright.
I still reside there by Dad's side,
bass fishing in the night.

I 'm still holding Daddies finger
back when I was two or three.
I'm still riding on Dads shoulders.
I am Love; My spirit's free.

God's gift of life dwells near the veil,
I'm now beyond life's tears,
in a place of peace, of joy, of love.
A wondrous place my after years.

I've passed thru the veil that binds us there,
no more war nor hell from man.
My passage thru our veil was quite okay,
a burst of love was there to greet me
and at last I understand.

This time after my life on earth,
I travel now on rays of time.
I gather joyful stardust from my past,
from those I've loved so very much,
from those I left behind.

My dog "Old Gent'" plays by my side
in this tranquil land beyond your sky.
He radiates our love from Childhood years;
For me, our country's Soldier Boy.
For I've a Soul that did not die.

Show moms torments when word is sent
her little boy has died.
Show sad tears flow and pain won't go,
show hurt there deep inside.

I implore again dead Warrior friends,
show freedoms are not free.
Show the dark side and do not hide
painful death and misery.

Show artillery pound as you hugged the ground,
show Warriors torn asunder.
Show spirits fly for peace in sky,
leaving shrapnel, hell and thunder.

Show us despair in men's eyes there,
just before they cloud.
Deaths wounds expose and show deaths throes
as men take on deaths shroud.

.Show sweet sickening smell of death from hell
as shrapnel slices Buddies down.
Show dripping parts and blown out hearts
and blood sucked up by ground.

Show death march north of Twenty-fourth
after the divisions ripped to shreds.
Show those of God who couldn't trod,
old Nuns and Priests all dead.

Show death camps there under "tigers" care
where starvation did abound.
Show "Johnson's List" the ones death kissed
and graves that won't be found.

Let us know of death in snow,
show grotesque shapes of frozen men.
Show frozen feet and then repeat
dead grotesque shapes again.

Young bodies froze in life's last throes,
camera clicks eternity.
For us that live please don't forgive
if we think freedoms free.

Show intestines ripped and hands that grip,
bloody fingers force them in.
He went thru this all for freedoms cause,
primordial scream —— amen.

Show wounds suck air from lung shot there,
show choking on life's blood.
His voice not found, just gurgle sounds,
show deaths from warring crud.

.Show men that run from death by gun,
show stark terror in their face.
Those not too daft will dodge the draft,
someone else must take their place.

In summers rain show torturous pain
where reeking bodies swell.
In summers heat show rotting meat
of Buddies blown to hell.

Show the damn flies we all despise,
show the maggots as they crawl.
Show all these things, make ignorant cringe
at the price of freedoms cause.

Show bayonets flash as the blades clash
in combat hand to hand.
Show life just wilt as to the hilt
blades stuck in gut of Warrior man.

Show blood run cold in your foxhole
as artillery slams you 'round.
Show damn air burst that was the worse,
mixed your blood and flesh with ground.

Show mustard gas as you breathed your last
in France in world war one.
Show lungs on fire, when one desire is air;
but life is done.

Show how you hold buddies near cold
as eternity draws near.
Show this my friend, how at the end
Some cry out for, Ma-Ma Dear.

.Line up your dead, show wounds blood red
since days of nations birth.
Dead shuffle along, one million strong,
show price of freedoms worth.

March down our streets, slow funeral beats,
your tortured dead from war.
Some aren't aware, most just don't care
'bout freedoms you died for.

Let out your groan, in deaths pain moan
as you limp by us the living.
Make uncaring see what's kept us free
deaths' debts of freedoms giving.

Surround those there who do not care,
make them view your pain dulled eyes.
Make them touch blood, wounds caked with mud,
demand they apologize.

I'll ask all why freedoms slide by
that I died for long ago.
Does no one care 'bout my death there?
No, long dead son; just let it go.

They won't understand they love this land,
we are now our country's' bane.
They'll take deaths shroud and form those clouds,
those clouds, dark "tears of rain."

Show our constitution and bill of rights
for which you died so long ago,
place them in the pool of blood
of your million dead or so.

.Dark clouds despair show all deaths there,
place above that pool of pain,
Force us to see what's kept us free,
your deaths, so freedoms would remain.

The sun shone thru after world war two
on the pool and constitution where
the golden light made glow what's right
and we in our land showed care.

Dark clouds close in and it's a sin,
our constitution fades toward gray.
In this land of mine it's tough to find
in this pool of blood a ray.

The ray is there, if enough care
our constitution will shine once more.
Protect it we must, fulfill our trust,
to those who died, our debts of war.

Open our eyes, our children's eyes
to your deaths long time in past.
You left in "trust" freedoms for us,
with uncaring it won't last.

The dead my friend won't rise again,
there can't be such a thing.
If they could I know they would
cry out; demand that freedoms ring.

I end this part with tired heart,
with sorrow and deep pain.
Good-bye my friends, dead Warrior friends
and welcome now dark "tears of rain."

This long line of our dead young Warriors, about one million strong, stretches back from time, to not just you and me, but most directly to those who represent us thru our free elections. Elected officials, local, state and especially the federal are the only ones who have the power to assure that dark clouds don't form, Tears of Rain won't fall.

jimmie joe,
fishhook junction, Alaska

Preamble to our Constitution

We the People of the United States, in Order to form a more perfect Union, establish Justice, insure domestic Tranquility, provide for the common defense, promote the general Welfare, and secure the Blessings of Liberty to ourselves and our Posterity, do ordain and establish this Constitution for the United States of America.

The (Our) Bill of Rights

Article I: Freedom of speech, religion, press, petition and assembly.
Article II: Right to bear arms and militia.
Article III: Quartering of soldiers.
Article IV: Warrants and searches.
Article V: Individual debt and double jeopardy.
Article VI: Speedy trial, witnesses and accusations.
Article VII: Right for a jury trial.
Article VIII: Bail and fines.
Article IX: Existence of other rights for the people.
Article X: Power reserved to the states and people.

Article I.

Congress shall make no law respecting an establishment of religion, or prohibiting the free exercise thereof; or abridging the freedom of speech, or of the press; or the right of the people peaceably to assemble, and to petition the Government for a redress of grievances.

Article II.

A well regulated Militia, being necessary to the security of a free State, the right of the people to keep and bear Arms, shall not be infringed.

Article III.

No Soldier shall, in time of peace be quartered in any house, without the consent of the Owner, nor in time of war, but in a manner to be prescribed by law.

Article IV.

The right of the people to be secure in their persons, houses, papers, and effects, against unreasonable searches and seizures, shall not be violated, and no Warrants shall issue, but upon probable cause, supported by Oath or affirmation, and particularly describing the place to be searched, and the persons or things to be seized.

Article V

No person shall be held to answer for a capital, or otherwise infamous crime, unless on a presentment or indictment of a Grand Jury, except in cases arising in the land or naval forces, or in the Militia, when in actual service in time of War or public danger; nor shall any person be subject for the same offence to be twice put in jeopardy of life or limb; nor shall be compelled in any criminal case to be a witness against himself, nor be deprived of life, liberty, or property, without due process of law; nor shall private property be taken for public use, without just compensation.

Article VI.

In all criminal prosecutions, the accused shall enjoy the right to a speedy and public trial, by an impartial jury of the State and district wherein the crime shall have been committed, which district shall have been previously ascertained by law, and to be informed of the nature and cause of the accusation; to be confronted with the witnesses against him; to have compulsory process for obtaining witnesses in his favor, and to have the Assistance of Counsel for his defence.

Article VII.

In Suits at common law, where the value in controversy shall exceed twenty dollars, the right of trial by jury shall be preserved, and no fact tried by a jury, shall be otherwise re-examined in any Court of the United States, than according to the rules of the common law.

Article VIII.

Excessive bail shall not be required, nor excessive fines imposed, nor cruel and unusual punishments inflicted.

Article IX.

The enumeration in the Constitution, of certain rights, shall not be construed to deny or disparage others retained by the people.

Article X.

The powers not delegated to the United States by the Constitution, nor prohibited by it to the States, are reserved to the States respectively, or to the people.

A Cause that's Just

A Cause that's Just" in my mind is a cause where we are defending our homeland from a foreign power with which America is at war, where our very survival is at risk. Another "Cause that's Just" may be the defense of South Korea after the North Koreans invaded on the Twenty-fifth of June, Nineteen-fifty.

With the defeat of the North Korean Army by November Nineteen-fifty the picture changed drastically. China warned our State Department that she would not stand for a super power on her border. There were skirmishes with the Red Chinese Army in Northeast Korea about the last of October 1950. China withdrew and waited.

At this time diplomacy should have taken over, Mac Arthur refused to heed this warning. He ordered the push on to the Yalu River. Mac Arthur was basically a God, to Americans and politicians alike.

Mac Arthur claimed China would not enter the war, I feel he lied, he wanted China in. It would be his last great campaign, freeing China from the Red Chinese. He spent his entire command career in the Orient; he knew the oriental mindset better than any military man.

We had intelligence on the ground about the buildup of Red Chinese forces. We had air superiority; we observed quite well the buildup across the Yale River. Our troops on the ground may have been taken by surprise by the Chinese hoards that smashed across the Yale River, Mac Arthur and certain others most assuredly were not.

The Politicians and State Department could have ended the war in October or November, they didn't. Whether from their own malfeasance or the total belief in Mac Arthur I don't know. I do know at this point our politicians failed in their sacred duty, we were no longer fighting for "A Cause that's Just". An extra two to three million Civilians died, about one million more warriors, all because of one general with an ego like a God and politicians with no courage except one, "Old Harry" and his showed up to late by ten months.

The proof of an unjust war is when a homeland no longer has a caring about the men involved in said war. A homeland that doesn't have the intelligence to comprehend it's the politicians who thru their failings cause the wars and then draft the most recent crop of young Boys to die in their "Just Cause". Young sacrifices, politician's renewable resources.

The war powers act should be eliminated; one man should not have the power to commit our armed forces without the support of Congress. It's insanity! You get Johnson's "Vietnam" and his damn "Gulf of Tonkin lie" believed and approved by Congress with only Greuning from Alaska and Morris from Oregon voting no!

Bush had his Panama and Clinton threw missiles at four different countries so far, all acts of war without congressional approval. A hell of a lot of humans have died so a president, a country or a General could "save Face", it's Bullshit.

View the film of some World War Two combat men who never did recover, who died in institutions as near zombies, they fought a "Just Cause" and still could not cope. This film was deemed to disturbing to be viewed by the general public and was never released. How can we expect young boys we send to war in a cause that is questionable to cope? How about the near totally unjust causes? How do we cope with unjust politicians?

There is a very important difference in how Warriors will adjust thru the years after the battles have ended; a "Just Cause" is that difference. View World War Two than view Vietnam.

It is imperative Warriors have a "Just Cause" to justify the carnage and death we witness, otherwise a lot of men's minds will not be able to accept or adjust. I speak of Warriors who were in actual combat for prolonged periods. — ——The Grunts

jimmie joe

A Cause that's Just

.Our last "true Just Cause" was World War Two
'near sixty years back in time.
To save this world most Warriors
knew it was worth their warring slime.

These men came home to cheering throngs,
the tired Warriors earned the cheers.
The next two wars when men returned
by their countrymen were spurned.

I'm not qualified to write of Vietnam,
about their war I will not tell.
Still I'm trying to tie together,
times of "all" our non-adjusting;
Of why our non-adjusting hell.

Our country didn't care about Korea,
about Vietnam they cared much less.
Their contempt and their uncaring,
left our "Just Cause" quite a mess.

A "Just Cause" is really needed
for the Warriors who survive.
In our heads we need a reason,
to free our ghosts of warring season.

A reason for foxhole Buddies
who didn't make it home.
A reason for dying Children
who as "Shadow Ghosts" still roam.

.A reason for a Congress
who said "stepped War's a go".
An extra fifty thousand dead in Vietnam
'cause Congress can't say no.

You looked on our wars as all quite small,
not real like World War Two.
As grim reaper struck our buddies down
there was no support from you.

America didn't seem to give a damn
about her fighting men.
They had their fill in World War two,
to this I say "Amen".

A bullet killed us just as dead,
hot jagged flying shrapnel too.
We still held dying Buddies
as you did in World War Two.

The only difference was a "Just Cause,
that was on your side.
You saved our Freedoms for us all
and you came home with pride.

You came home to millions of
cheering parties all across this land.
We came home to silence.
No, "thank you boy"; No band.

We didn't win in Korea
and your Warriors you would blame.
There was no all out war 'gainst China,
"Politicians take your shame."

.Vietnam Vets came home to bastards
who spit on some Warrior men.
They came home to worse than silence.
Some spewed hate — Amen.

We pushed North Korea to the Yale River
Nineteen fifty in November.
We won the war in just five months,
then China hit and none remember.

We fought and died in numbers great,
South Korea we had freed.
We would have been home by Christmas.
Politicians let China intercede.

Mac Arthur wanted one last laurel
to be pinned upon his chest.
Free China from the commies
and he tried his level best.

All of China was Mac Arthur's goal,
too late Truman set him right.
We were already engaging China
in a bloody winter fight.

That's the trouble with Infantry
when politicians do not try,
we're the ones who have to cope.
We're the ones who die.

Naive were we and Warriors young,
who thought our country always right.
At first we thought our Cause was just,
took years to see the light.

.We fought them to a stand off,
the War ended in a tie.
For one damn General's ego
a few million more would die.

After November of Nineteen-fifty
all of the Korean wars long dead,
by a count of several million
rest on politicians heads.

We believed in God and country.
We believed in Mom and apple pie.
We believed in Causes that were Just.
We believed the bastards lies.

Pride for many years evaded us,
none was shown us here at home.
No gratitude to fill our minds
to displace the "Ghosts" who roam.

The Korean Warriors said nothing,
our battles we did store.
Deep back inside a pain filled wall
was our Forgotten War.

It was forgotten by our countrymen,
forgotten by our Kin.
It hid inside our Warriors heads.
No Just Cause; Our hidden sin?

The Korean War stayed hidden well,
'til we had Internet in our homes.
Then we found we weren't the only ones
with those "Ghosts of War" that roam.

.Because of Vietnam's Gulf of Tonkin lie
under Johnson's tender care.
Many thousands of our Warriors died,
many Vets have vacant stare.

A lot of Vets adjust just fine
but the homeless I can't name,
the ones who wander thru this land
are proof of our country's shame.

The "Just cause" the warriors needed
was nowhere to be found.
How can we justify the pain and dying
of all our Comrades in the ground?

Again we believed in God and country.
We believed in Mom and apple pie.
We believed in "Causes that were Just".
Why did we believe their lies?

Congress has the power to make the rules
about "A Cause that's Just".
Since World War Two they've not done well,
in malfeasance they do trust.

Adjusting to carnage and death
is tough enough to do,
it's only hopelessness that's left
when homeland spits on you.

We're done, we'll leave, we're out of here.
We'll go we don't know where.
The hell with you, we'll disappear,
you sent us over there.

.There are a lot of homeless veterans
who wander thru this land.
Looking for an answer,
to help them understand.

jimmie joe

A Cause that's Just they were denied
by our politicians here.
Our reasons for Comrades who died?
Our reasons disappeared.

Adjusting isn't easy
when men first come home from war.
Adjusting isn't easy
when these young men you ignore.

When you spit on us and hate us,
this hurt we're forced to hide.
In back of mind with other hurts,
those War hurts deep inside.

Please don't do it,
our minds already sore.
You sent us off to War.

To a War without "A Cause that's Just"?
a War built on politicians lies.
That little "Gulf of Tonkin" fuss
caused millions more to die.

Politicians should carry all the blame
for pain and guilt from "Unjust Wars".
Instead they have no answer.
We're not needed any more.

America will back "A Cause that's Just"
and politicians please take note,
.we deplore you for our unjust Wars.
We deplore you with no vote.

We deplore you for our Buddies
and all the innocent who've died.
We deplore you for not caring
about our lives, our pain, our pride.

We deplore not stopping Mac Arthur
'till he had drawn the Chinese in.
We deplore you for "Gulf of Tonkin" lie,
We Damn you for these sins.

For you we went to battle.
Because of you our Buddies died,.
Died for you in unjust cause.
How many Mothers cried?

Because of you we have our homeless.
For thirty years our streets they roam.
It's too late now to help them.
Too late you said "Son Welcome Home".

The p.t.s.d. type of our homeless
are difficult to verify.
Too many wannabe's on our streets
who never saw their Comrades die.

I only rhyme about our combat vets,
the phonies I disdain.
I only care about the Vets
who faced wars death and pain.

Adjusting some just cannot do
they never stood a prayer.
On the streets they'll live and die alone
because their country didn't care.

I don't blame them, I'm blaming you,
the VA, congress and me too.
Had we given them A Cause that's Just,
their numbers would be few.

Counselors today are everywhere,
They converge on every tragic scene.
For each traumatic exposure
near civilians they are seen.

I think this is needed and fine
but this caring is quite new.
They went thru trauma just one time
not for a year or two.

Our adjusting we had to face alone,
there was no counseling long ago.
A few inside their minds did not come home,
their minds still hold what you don't know.

Alone we drift to VA counseling
and we drift back out again.
For our "unjust cause" we get no answer,
No answer? our subconscious sin?.

Next we visit the VA hospital
for help to ease the pain.
To the physic ward we stop a while
and the Bastards fry our brain.

We give up!, there is no help,
our answer can't be found.
We go back to the street and cardboard boxes,
not quite ready for the ground.

Now drugs and alcohol fry our brain
and numb the Ghosts we hide.
They take away the nagging pain,
give back some phony pride.

Kinda makes us feel okay
with a full bottle in our shed.
Hides those Ghosts, those long dead Ghosts,
that sneak out from our head.

I'll make it thru the day,
just a little drink or two.
Maybe heroin in the vein
or coke or crack will do.

It kind of takes away my pain.
It makes me feel all right.
See those dark clouds? Those Tears of Rain.
Hope it doesn't rain tonight.

We fought and died for you America
and your Warriors you will curse?
Our buddies dying hurt quite deep
but your attitude hurts worse.

That's the life we gave to Vets
The "Unjust War" syndrome.
Not all, but some truly needed;
"Good to see you Welcome Home".

Your "Cause was Just" my Warrior friend,
the damn politicians lied.
If you fought their war with Honour,
than hold up your head with pride.

If you helped the little Children
in that far off warring land.
Hold up your head with Honour,
us Grunts all understand.

If you held a dying Buddy
as he took on deaths shroud.
Hold up your head with Honour
of you us Grunts are proud.

If you despise carnage and death,
be it friend or be it foe,
Hold up your head with Honour,
you're a Just man us Grunts know.

To hell with politicians lies;
to hell with Unjust wars.
If you fought their lying war with Honour.
God will not ask for more.

jimmie joe
fishhook junction, alaska

A Cause that's Just?

South Korean soldiers and police executed more than 2,000 political prisoners without trial in the early weeks of the Korean War.

It causes outrage to me as some executions were observed by American Army officers who didn't have the honour to stop it, or possibly they did try and couldn't. Mac Arthur could have, the State Department could have and Truman sure as hell could have.

The statistics below are from are from a "Washington Post" investigative report and would be minuscule of the true number of atrocities committed against hapless Civilians. Four different times the battles raged thru the central section of Korea, four times Civilians were caught up in the waves of massacres. I'll grant the North Koreans committed most atrocities but the South Korean army and police apparently committed a vast number.

We will never know the true numbers, I find in what I can dig up estimates ranging from two to six million Civilians died in the war, either number is an abomination on all who participated in the intentional murdering of innocent Humans.

There is not a need of it or any excuse those kinds of bastards can give, it is genocide and a crime against Humanity. Hell all wars are politician's failures, all are crimes against Humanity. The soldiers committing atrocities are no more despicable than the politicians who stage the war.

Gen. Douglas Mac Arthur was aware of some of the mass shootings, according to documents classified "top secret" and released thru our freedom of information act.

HYPERLINK "http://about.delphi.com/n/main.asp?webtag=ab-usmilitary&nav=messages&msg=2092.1"

Hundreds of civilians were put aboard ships, taken out to sea, shot and their bodies dumped overboard. Mac Arthur commanded the South Korean military at the time; he referred this report on its actions to American diplomats "for consideration" and "such action as you consider appropriate."

.American witnesses reported that 200 to 300 prisoners, including women and a girl 12 or 13 years old, were killed by South Korean military police on Aug. 10, 1950. Korean soldiers placed 20 prisoners at a time on the edge of a cliff and shot them in the back of the head, some did not die immediately. Three hours after the executions were completed, some of the condemned Humans were still alive and moaning.

U.S. Army attaché Lt. Col. Bob E. Edwards reported that 1,800 political prisoners were executed over three days at Taejon.

It pained my soul to learn my war was so corrupted by the actions of the South. I had much soul searching and many questions about the civilian casualties resulting from our bombing of the North Korean cities. I now must add South Koreas criminal conduct, with our knowledge, and ask WHY did we allow it to happen.

My war has become very different with passage of time because of the historical documents time revealed, it is quite sad. *I must repeat;*

Damn the worlds politicians, the safe, fat, contemptuous, flag waving bastards who consider war a crime against Humanity as something only the loser can commit. The egotistical asses never even consider that war itself is a crime against Humanity.

Justice truly is blind.

God alone knows the number murdered by the North Korean Reds or the South Korean dictatorships military and police. After we entered North Korea near Hague a prison was torched by the retreating Red army, burning alive the hundreds of prisoners inside. The murdering bastards executed several hundred old Men, Women and Children in a ditch near town.

Outside town at the base of a cliff was a pile of Human remains fifty to a hundred feet high, the bones near the bottom were quite old, near the top quite new. All this in one small area of Korea, God alone knows the total for the entire country. I remember a group of townsmen armed with axes, hoes and clubs marching a large group of their oppressors out of town to what I presumed to be their execution. When we were beaten back by the Chinese a few months later I would guess the avengers met the same fate.

Our three-years of bombing North Korea also contributed greatly to the terrible carnage of innocent deaths.

War equals bombs, then comes the starvation and disease. Thru it from the start come the massacres, the rapes, the suicides and all manners of carnage against the innocent. I pray the bastards and the humane will be well sorted on judgment day with justice for all.

jimmie joe

Atonement—?

Atonement is a quite complicated state of mind to achieve. If I have been able to atone thru my writings it has to have been with help from God, a God I have never been able to grasp and believe in the way I feel I should.

I never killed the wounded, the undefended enemy or civilians. I have seen literally hundreds of old men, women and Children who had been massacred by the North Korean, and possibly (the South Korean army as I learned fifty years later). As we headed north I viewed the maimed survivors from our bombing of the North Korean cities.

Somehow I have felt a degree of guilt about these deaths, deaths I had nothing to do with. How does one atone for the enemies or his own country's' methods of warfare? The burden is great and complicated for one Grunt.

Throughout our wars there have been an abhorrent number of dead innocents. Between two and six million civilians died in Korea and roughly one and a half to two million soldiers. Fifty years later the number of civilian deaths is still growing due to the North Korean regime. Starvation and disease, which are a large cause of death in any war, is still occurring in North Korea, all from a war of fifty years ago. There are so many countries on this earth where, the fact of just being born there, Humans seem predestined to a life of suffering and early miserable death.

Atonement? I try, but don't know. I've done the best I can.

jimmie joe
fishhook junction, alaska

Atonement

I end these rhymes of warring times
'cause Ghosts I have set free.
I've ended pain locked in my brain
from my days across the sea.

My mind had control 'til I grew old
and retired all alone.
With just me home the Ghosts would roam.
The booze did not atone.

Near fifty years I'd suppressed tears,
manly men don't cry.
I'm here to tell I cried like hell.
My choices? — Cry or die.

The Shadow Ghosts who'd been my host
since times long in the past,
thru rhymes by me are now set free.
Shadows no more they cast.

Children's haunting eyes for years despised
have softened now to Love.
They hold my hand in peaceful land,
I thank our Lord above.

Buddies long dead have left my head
and rest where they belong.
Where pain did swell just sadness dwells
'bout ending young life's song.

No more do rhymes cause tearful times,
my soul's typed out it's grief.
I'm glad I'm thru; Bet you are too,
old Warrior's had his Ghost relief.

I hope readers see what's kept us free,
tho rhymes may not be first rate.
Men died for you and the next line's true.
Our Freedoms had a Bloody Mate.

jimmie joe,
fishhook junction, alaska

Our treatment of Vietnam Vets.
"America's Shame"

They sleep and die in door ways,
it bothers us as we walk by.
We wish they'd just go away,
their disgraceful to our eyes.

We don't care for decrepit warriors
or their non adjusting fears.
What kind of fighting men were you?
Hell, it's been 'most thirty years!

So we'll leave them to die alone
with their hepatitis "C"
or maybe aids from needles shared
or maybe they'll just freeze.

It doesn't matter how they die,
they'll be away from you and me.
When their spirits soar for peace in sky,
then all their Ghosts will flee.

A forlorn spot in paupers field,
no tombstone marks his grave.
"A mound of earth NOW's all he's worth."
His country's warrior brave.

It's hard to believe that derelict
fought a war to keep us free.
It's hard to give that man respect,
hell, he's not like you or me.

He was once, about thirty years ago,
he came back from war, did his bloody tour.
Good bye young man; Get out, go home,
it's warm above the sewer.

A cardboard box is good enough,
You're now a "Vet" === Hell man you're tough.

jimmie joe
fishhook junction, alaska

The end result of our treatment of Vietnam Vets.
"America's Shame"

Those young Boys from Vietnam, fresh out of horrors most people will never see, were treated as no other servicemen in America's history. The pains many of them still carry are a direct result of their treatment by America's young. Mobs would harass them on their return from combat, calling them baby killers and spitting their spittle and shouting their hate.

Riots against the war took place at the democratic convention in Chicago in 1968; this action was well justified for those convinced the war was unjust. It should have been carried to the halls of congress and into the oval office, not against our Warriors.

Our homeless Vietnam Vets are the direct result of their treatment upon their return from war and for years after. Politicians gave us what some considered an "unjust war" and the troops were blamed by ignorant asses, most have no concept of the lives they are responsible for destroying, the number of suicides they have caused. Suicides which continue and — continue and — and continue — and continue — over 200,000 and counting! As of 1998.

jimmie joe
fishhook junction, alaska

173

Memorial Day, 2001,

24th. Inf. Div., 34th. /21st Inf. Reg. — 1950/51

I thank my fallen Comrades and it matters not if they fell at Valley Forge, the North or South in our Civil War, nor any War, be it as large as World War II or as small as peacekeeping in the Balkans. It matters not if they fell in a War some of our Countrymen believe was wrong, or a War "I" believe not just and it matters not if they fell in a training accident.

It matters not if a Cross, a Star of David, a Crescent Moon, or any other inscription carved in stone identifies their mound of earth, and it matters not the Race of the one who rests below.

These have nothing to do with the honour I bestow on our men and women who die in harms way, and they have nothing to do with how I feel on a Day such as this. Memorial Day brings back sadness with a bit of pain, I am reminded there is a infinitely more pain carried for a lifetime by the Moms, Dads, Wives, Children and all who love their Warrior dead.

One-day a year set aside for remembrance is minuscule, enjoy your long weekend but please take a moment for a prayer of thanks.

I honour you my Warrior Brothers,
I'll join you in a while.
Will you welcome me as Comrade brave?
or will there be no smile?

Have I upheld your sacrifice and death
as I lived time you never had?
Is our Homeland as Free as when you left?
By "Gods own truth" your answer is ————?
Your answer friend ———— is mine.

Although our Warriors were young men, in my olden mind we were Boys, with much honour and respect I shall refer to them as such throughout my writings, those Boys were damn fine Men.

jimmie joe,
fishhook junction, alaska

.jimmie joe's thoughts of Bastards

Newly disclosed documents suggest that as many as 900 U.S. servicemen were left behind in North Korea after the United States and North Korea exchanged prisoners following the Korean War. The Dwight D. Eisenhower Presidential Library released the declassified papers.

The public didn't know about those left behind, but it is clear that Eisenhower did. Five months after the war, in a document dated December 22, 1953, Army Secretary Robert Stevens met with President Eisenhower and told him the Defense Department had the names of 610 Army people and over 300 Air Force prisoners still held by the North Koreans.

A number of people confirmed the reports, citing their own experiences. Retired Colonel Phillip Corso, a former intelligence aide to Eisenhower, watched the exchange of prisoners at Panmunjon, and talked with some of those who came back. "Our own boys told me there were sick and wounded American boys not 10 miles from the camp, and they were not exchanged," he said.

A former Czechoslovakian general and Soviet intelligence agent, Jan Sejna, defected to the United States before the end of the Cold War. He told Congress Tuesday that he saw some of the prisoners being used in gruesome medical experiments. "The top-secret purpose of the hospital was medical experimentation on Americans and South Koreans. The POWs were used to test the effects of chemical and biological weapons, and test the effects of atomic radiation," Sejna said. "The Soviets also used the American prisoners to test the psychological endurance of American soldiers. They were also used to test various mind controls.

The Eisenhower documents suggest that although that administration was concerned about the possibility that it had abandoned POWs, it did not make the issue public for fear of a nuclear confrontation with Russia or China.

our betrayed

Nine hundred ten who fought for us
in korea and were captured long ago,
were abandoned to a dreadful fate
this traitorous act at last we know.

Those men we left, we left to death
and tortures we can't comprehend.
My country in my mind won't find
atonement for those warriors end.

For us they fought and 'twas for naught,
in untold pain they all have died.
Politicians back then betrayed our men,
where is their honor? where is pride?

We were well aware that they were there,
politicians and some generals too.
I can't believe how they deceive,
for politicians that's not new.

My heart does weep, fury runs deep,
the bastards left our combat men.
None seem to care and I'm aware
given time it will be done again.

Politicians lies I just despise,
their deception isn't rare.
To date it's such a common trait
and so few in this land care.

Our founding fathers would rebel
against our government today.
They'd wish the bastards into hell
and help them on their way.

jimmie joe

Our Korean war POWs

During The infamous Bataan death march of World War Two and the subsequent imprisonment our POWs, nearly four years later 52% survived. They came home and were greeted as heroes and rightfully so.

The average survival rate of our POWs under Japanese control was 74%, under German control 96%, and POWs of the Korean War, who after up to three years in captivity only 49% survived to make it home. Somewhere in there were over eight thousand of our MIAs that if counted would make the survival rate a deplorable 20%, yet we hear absolutely nothing of this. The difference seems to be Americas attitude about anything connected with the war in Korea, as if the war never took place!

As far back as 1953, retired Lieutenant General James A. Van Fleet, who had commanded the U.S. 8th Army in Korea (and whose son was among the POW/MIAs), was quoted in the New York Times as saying that "a large percentage of the over 8,000 American soldiers listed as missing in action are still alive."

Van Fleet was not alone in this assessment. General Mark Clark, former U.S. commander in Korea, upon his sudden resignation from Army in 1953, accused the communists of holding several thousand American servicemen after the prisoner switches supposedly had been completed. But even such blunt comments from well-respected leaders evoked no results; indeed, the remarks were soon forgotten and America went on feeling quite good about herself.

A few POWs "turned" thru brainwashing by the Reds, a methodology unknown in our militaries prior history. None were prepared or trained to cope with this unknown. America and the military did a great and uncalled for injustice to the survivors of the communist death camps.

Because of the few who succumbed a pall was cast over all. Too few Americans answered the unjust critics. This must have been a time of great distress to those brave Warriors. After going thru years of hellish inhumane treatment where over half their Buddies died America put them thru polluted bullshit and treated them all like the few that turned.

Near fifty years have passed and many of these survivors are still receiving counseling. In a part some this is due to their treatment by America thru the months and years after their return. It took years before the degree of treatment was recognized as needed, by the Veteran himself or by the VA.

I cannot apologize for America. I will apologize for myself. When I came home from the ongoing war in Korea I tried to shut the war out, I ignored it, except in my dreams. It would flit in and out but I kept it hidden as best I could, until nineteen ninety-seven when I read the Eisenhower Papers. I couldn't believe what I read; I had to believe what was to me unbelievable. The documentation is there in those damn "Secret files", released 28 years after Eisenhower's death in 1969.

Cold rage slowly built up with the realization that my country could/would do this to her Warriors, rage at the news media that gave it very little coverage, rage at America then and those who don't care now, disappointment in myself for not facing the reality of the Korean War. I should have been more involved with my comrades in arms. I am ashamed for all the years I spent in the limbo of self-imposed ignorance of forgetting and offered no helping hand to my Brothers who faced so much more than I, so much more than I can even imagine.

All POWs who survived the death camps of North Korea are very exceptional people. The will and courage to keep putting one foot ahead of the other day after day for up to three years while coping with cold, malnutrition, dysentery, mental and physical torture and watching over half their Buddies die, have been and are to this day truly Heroic survivors.

I Honour you my friends, I pray God will grant you the Peace of mind we denied you. Forgive me.

jimmie joe

I despise the politicians without honour who abandoned our Warriors. Eisenhower was not the only one, our other political leaders, our State Department and some of our own military must have known. In reality we were and always have been their expendable "tin soldiers" whose courage on the battleground was always demanded in the name of Liberty, Loyalty, God and Country. Loyalty: A one-way street to torture, death and abandonment via the route of political expediency while the traitorous bastards wave Our Flag for votes. The very Flag they have desecrated thru abandonment of those who took the risks for our freedoms. Wave it at political rallies and tell us how we have the greatest country in the world. Ask the men we knowingly left to a fate known only to God and our enemies, tell me again about our country and it's greatness. Our Constitution is where the greatness has, does and will live. What politicians do with it is ————————

You damn politicians and you of the fourth estate who fail to uncover and publish all the facts revealing dastardly acts of our politicians and you damn Americans who could care less. Where were your outrage, your disbelief, and your demand for laws that would make these sorts of things an act of treason?

We knowingly left men in Russia after World War Two. In Korea memos to Eisenhower verified our Boys were left behind, their government abandoned the crews of planes that went down in areas of the Soviet sphere of influence during the cold war. Vietnam also had many Boys left to their fate, a fate known only to God. Our young Warriors offer up their lives for our freedoms and with disdain we discard their sacrifice as not worthy of further allegiance.

What the hell kind of country have we allowed ourselves to become? The innocent millions who died from starvation, disease and bombs in Korea and Vietnam, the hundreds killed in Panama. We've bombed Serbia and Kosovo leaving several thousand more dead, please note we've never been told actual numbers.

We send tomahawk missiles into the Sudan and Afghanistan with no declaration of war, a sneak attack. Remember Pearl Harbor?

We are good at spreading death and destruction with high technology; we are very poor at spreading peace thru our wisdom and compassion. Damn the politicians and Fourth Estate who praise my Buddies on the eleventh hour of the eleventh day of the eleventh month and spend three hundred sixty-four days a year dismantling that for which our veterans have fought and died.

jimmie joe

The ones in power slowly devour
the freedoms for which men died,.
The enemy's not 'cross the seas,
inside the beltway they abide

Sacred Arlington

This Honour for our Arlington was a result of the nineteen ninety-seven internment of an unqualified political crony of President Clinton. Accurate records are a must for internment in Arlington, Clintons cronies were lacking. The grave had a rather large pink marble headstone was placed in front of the Congressional Medal of Honour recipients small white headstones and nearest President Kennedy's eternal flame.

It disturbed me greatly to have Arlington desecrated this way. I hadn't even known I cared, but apparently I care very deeply and I don't know why but I am saddened and quite angry by events.

In hallowed ground our warriors sleep
some with loved ones by their sides.
the living visit here, some weep,
while others cry inside.

Some died in combat; Died too young
protecting you and me.
Their "song of life" had just begun.
Brave men have kept us free.

We owe a debt we can't repay
to these men, these bits of clay.
We owe a debt we can't repay.
God bless these Moms who kneel and pray.

There is one deed that we can do
make politicians all agree,
only vets shall rest in hallowed ground
once owned by General Lee.

.Some NOW claim to buy the right
in this sacred ground to rest.
Their political donations

will not pass our warriors test.
Who takes from us our hallowed ground
where Warriors spirits hover near?
Only those whose rights abound
shall be buried here.

Politicians make the rules
'bout who gets out or in.
Waivers handed out by fools
displace some Warrior men.

How did congress earn the right
to rest in our sacred ground?
Thru passing laws? a political fight?
their self-importance does astound.

Many have fought their way thru wars
some lived and some would "die".
Deprive them of this sacred ground
and Warrior Spirits will cry.

I can't believe the pain I feel
when non-vets are interned there.
I can't believe the pain I feel
I did not know I would care.

This sacred ground, this Honored Clay,
It's not a game damn you; Don't play!
This ground holds its warriors dear.
Only Warriors shall rest here.

.I did not think our "Arlington"
was a special place to me.
I'd fought in war and near Pusan
I earned my c.i.b.

At unknown Soldier they lay a wreath,
small tear comes to my eye.
Sacrilege at "Arlington" brings grief.
It makes this grown man cry, I have no idea why?

Subconscious mind can hide away
the sights and pains of warring days,
but as the months or years slide past,
the piper will be pain at last.

We've paid the piper many times,
with our memories of war,
of buddies we have left behind,
of visions we abhor.

Please don't corrupt our sacred ground.
our Warriors Heaven's Gate.
We will not let this insult rest.
We'll be the hands of fate.

Contempt should sweep across this land
for politicians such as you,
most of you will never understand
why we feel the way we do.

I hope there will be a tidal wave
from seas to shining seas.
I hope forty million Veterans rave
and drive you to your knees.

I'll keep my eye upon the polls
with which you seem to sway.
I hope you'll regret you were so bold
trading our sacred ground away.

I've saw the "bastards" burn my flag
had anger past belief.
You trade away our sacred ground
brings pain, sad tears and grief.
Let a veteran lay the wreath!

For buddies who are not around
who did not make it home,
we've let our country slip to hell.
I don't know how I can atone.
few seem to care; I feel alone.

The cemeteries put in reserve
for Veterans tried and true.
"politicians stay away",
they never were and are not for
the likes of you.

jimmie joe

More then three months have gone
since I wrote the rhymes above,
it kind of seems like I was wrong
about people in this land I love.

There were a few it seemed to hurt,
it pained their Soul quite bad.
To most? Hell man; it's only dirt,
sometimes life's a bit sad.

.Little anger spread across this land
to most was no big deal.
Donate ten million dollars?
In sacred ground get sealed.

I thank the ones who raised the hell,
the ones who showed they care.
I thank the ones who raised the hell,
you got him dug out of there.

A draft dodger never really cares
about a Warriors sacred land.
The power of his politics
is all he understands.

I wonder how many others
rest there thru politicians grace?
I wonder how many others
took some brave Warriors place.

I really thought our veterans
would have made a bigger fuss.
Maybe not for them alone,
but for Buddies who didn't make it home.
The ones who died across the sea,
"Arlington's" their sacred memory.

I guess I'm thru; No more to rhyme,
for those who care; Have a nice time.
jimmie joe fishhook junction, alaska

Congress has tightened up the oversight on those who apply for internment is this sacred ground. No investigation was made into this political sacrilege against our Honored Dead. Perhaps it isn't rare but it most certainly approaches Sacrilege.

Johnson's List

Wayne Archer "Johnnie" Johnson, L Company, 21st Infantry Regiment, 24th Infantry Division, U. S. Army, was captured on July 11, 1950. Johnson became part of the Tiger Survivors group and was held for nearly 38 months by the North Koreans and the Chinese Army. He is from Lima, Ohio.

Johnson started keeping a record of the men who died in his camp so that the families back home would know what happened to their loved ones. The fact that he could have been punished or even shot for keeping such a list did not stop him. Along the way, buddies would tell him about someone dying and others would stand guard while Johnson recorded the deaths. See URL.

HYPERLINK ". < http://www.tigersurvivors.org/"
http://www.tigersurvivors.org/ >

I wanted Johnny's list to be
included here within my rhymes.
I wanted to let my Children see
some men that died near Boyhood time.

The names are people young and real,
Dad was their age back then.
I would like them in their hearts to feel
gratitude and thank these Warrior men.

They did await an awful fate
at the hands of North Korean Reds.
They struggled forth on death march north
before their saga ended most were dead.

Records now tell of Suffering hell,
their torturous pain of long ago.
By luck not prayer, Dad wasn't there,
their awful fate he wouldn't know.

Jim Woods, 34th./21st. inf. RCT

.In sad reflection — We did not know

To all "prisoners of war" we may never hear about whom have been "abandoned by our politicians" in our wars, this includes our "cold war" with the Soviet Union and World War II (left in the Soviet Union at the end of the war, we knew damn it, we knew they were left and did nothing.).

Korea (Known POWs left nine hundred and ten; two to four train loads of POWs sighted heading north out of Korea by several sources), POWs were used for experimental purposes as far away as Czechoslovakia and as near as the Yalu river; sworn statements by a former Czechoslovakian general before a Senate sub-committee, some of his sworn statements are bloodcurdling. God alone knows the fate of the 8,200 MIAs from the Korean War.

Vietnam claims there are no POWs retained in their country, there are about 2,500 MIAs unaccounted for from their war.

I doubt if any POWs have survived all these years, we must still strive for an accounting and we must never again allow our country to abandon our Warriors we send into harms way.

<

HYPERLINK "http://www.kimsoft.com/korea/mia-russ.htm"
http://www.kimsoft.com/korea/mia-russ.htm
HYPERLINK "http://www.kimsoft.com/korea/mia-us1.htm"
http://www.kimsoft.com/korea/mia-us1.htm

>

Below is the possible fate of some who defended America.
[I don't know if the General Sejna's sworn statement is trustworthy.]
Statement of Jan Sejna
Before the Subcommittee on Military Personnel
Of the House National Security Committee
September 17, 1996

At the end of the Korean War, there were about 100 POWs who were still considered useful for further experiments. I believe all others had been killed in the process of the experiments because I do not recall ever reading any report that indicated that any of the POW patients at the hospital left the hospital alive—except the 100 that were still alive at the end of the war. These 100 were flown in four groups first to Czechoslovakia, where they were given physical exams, and then onto the Soviet Union. I learned about all this from the Czech doctors who ran the hospital, from the Czech military intelligence officer in charge of the Czech operations in Korea, from Soviet advisors, and from official documentation that I reviewed in the process of responding to a Soviet request for Czechoslovakia to send medical doctors to the Soviet Union to participate in various experiments being run on the POWs who had been transferred to the Soviet Union. I also reviewed reports on the results of autopsies of the POWs, and received briefings on various aspects of the experiments

(See URL) <

HYPERLINK "http://www.nationalalliance.org/senja.htm"

>

During both the Korean and Vietnam Wars, the Soviet Union, assisted by Czechoslovakia, used over a thousand American POWs as guinea pigs in military medical intelligence experiments.

Experiments were run to determine the limits of physiological and psychological stress the captive GIs could endure. The Soviets justified these tests, Sejna explained, on the need to determine how well the Americans could stand up to the rigors of all-out war.

American and South Korean and South Vietnamese POWs were exposed to chemical warfare agents and biological warfare organisms to test their susceptibility to the different agents and organisms. The Soviets wanted to learn if the American GIs were any more, or less, vulnerable than the Soviet soldiers to the experimental agents they were developing. The Soviets also wanted to know if there were any differences between the races—black, white, Hispanic and Asian—in their biochemical vulnerability to the agents.

The captive GIs were also used as subjects in testing the effectiveness of military intelligence drugs, including a wide variety of mind-control and behavior-modification drugs, which, incidentally, were used during the Korean War to cause American servicemen to speak out on the evils of capitalism and on the benefits of communism.

The Soviets exposed GIs to atomic radiation to determine how much radiation was needed to kill or incapacitate a man. Tests to determine the long-term consequences of sub-lethal dose levels also were run. Lethal doses were administered and then the GIs were watched to determine how long soldiers could function and to learn if there were any drugs that could be used to prolong their ability to perform military tasks before permanently succumbing to the radiation.

Finally, autopsies were performed on the servicemen who did not survive the experiments to determine ethnic differences in biochemical makeup and to verify the effects of different drugs and biological organisms on the body, the heart and brain in particular.

Czechoslovakia's participation began early in the Korean War. The Soviets directed the Czechs to build an experimental hospital in North Korea. Ostensibly, the hospital was built to test new medical procedures for treating military casualties and for training young military doctors. This was its overt mission.

Covertly, the hospital served as a test bed in which captive American and South Korean servicemen were used as guinea pigs in the types of medical experiments described above. The Czechs also built a crematorium in North Korea to dispose of the remains. Sejna discussed the operation with the deputy director of military intelligence for strategic intelligence who was in charge of intelligence operations in North Korea at the time and with the doctor who actually ran the experimental hospital in North Korea.

The hospital was designed to handle two hundred "patients." In operation, the hospital was often overcrowded. One year six hundred patients were treated. The hospital was so crowded that two patients were often required to share one bed. Sejna never encountered any indication in any report or discussion that suggested that any of these hundreds of POW "patients" were ever returned back to the North Koreans.

In 1954, after the armistice was in effect, the Soviets decided to terminate operations in North Korea and turn the hospital over to the North Koreans. The roughly one hundred remaining American POWs were shipped back to the Soviet Union for long-term and more sophisticated experiments. For example, one of the experiments was to determine the long-term effects of sub-lethal doses of atomic radiation. To the Soviets, "long-term" usually meant several decades; fifty years was typical. In the case of the sub-lethal radiation effects, the Soviet interest included effects of radiation on the soldiers' reproductive organs and on their subsequent children and grandchildren.

The POWs were shipped by air, with a stop over in Prague, where the GIs were first examined for fitness before being sent on to various experimental medical test facilities in the Soviet Union. The stop over lasted typically about a week. The purpose of the stop over was for security to "break the trail" so that the Soviets could subsequently deny any claims that POWs were shipped to the U.S.S.R. from North Korea. This is also why the experimental hospital was a "Czech" hospital. These deceptions were all part of a carefully designed plan to mask the movement of GIs to the Soviet Union and mislead people about what was really happening and who was responsible. (For complete report on Senate Select Committee see URL) <
HYPERLINK "http://www.aiipowmia.com/reports/dglssmalfe.html"
http://www.aiipowmia.com/reports/dglssmalfe.html
>
This URL will cause you a great deal of sadness and anger.

jim woods

Russians, Americans still can't find Cold War prisoners

The Americans are particularly interested in the Korean War, when Moscow and North Korea had close ties. 8,177 Americans remain missing in action from that conflict.

The U.S. delegation has also sought information on American pilots who disappeared, nearly two hundred, while on spying mission over the Soviet Union. Ten spy planes were shot down between 1950 and 1965 and about 90 crewmen from the spy planes alone have not been accounted for. We denied the flights and we denied their existence.

The families of some Americans believe the MIAs from the Korean War were taken to the Soviet Union, and think some may still be alive in Russia. There in no evidence of any live Americans.

The Americans were given access to some classified Soviet-era documents, and interviewed current and former Russian military personnel. (For complete article see URL below)

"http://www.nando.net/newsroom/ntn/world/070197/world17_24110.html

In sad reflection — We did not know

Declassified government memos after forty-three years in the governments secret files show that top U.S. officials, including President Eisenhower, knew about the verified reports that POWs were still being held in the North Korea.

But the officials, the government, our government who my comrade's had gone to war to defend, fearful of touching off a nuclear holocaust in the tense Cold War of the early 1950s, decided against pressing the issue. Fear of nuclear war was the reasoning.

HYPERLINK "http://personalpages.tds.net/~kknowlto/barbed3.htm"

The following poem is for the minimum of nine and ten hundred American "POW's" who were "abandoned by our politicians" on July 27th. 1953 at a North Korean POW camp less than ten miles from the peace talks at Panmunjon Korea. (Eisenhower papers, released in 1996. via freedom of information act.)

flag—country—honor?

For fifty years now more or less
you've hid dishonor from the press.
American people must not know
that politicians stoop this low.

One more fact that I must note
politicians need your vote.
So they sacrificed our men
they promised us the war would end.

The war did end just like they said.
It's tough to deal with commie red.
They were elected once again
all because the war did end.

They don't think they're full of shit
cause they really put an end to it.
They ended honor, ended pride,
deep within their graves they hide.

The maggots in their carcass gorge
upon dishonor. — hell's their forge.

jimmie joe
fishhook junction, alaska

No Gun Ri

November 21, 1999

I have a friend who was a participant in this action; there is no way he recalls the death of those civilians as a massacre in the sense of a cold-blooded execution. I believe his recollection is correct, as he has lived with it every day for going on fifty years. I will point out times in my experiences where someone, green and under-trained for battle, panicked.

Late August nineteen-fifty; A warm cloudy night with a misty rain and pitch black, I am off guard duty and laying under my rain poncho which I had made onto a half shelter behind my foxhole. I had just dozed off when all hell broke loose; I rolled into my foxhole to total silence.

One of our green replacements had let his imagination get out of control, was all turned around in the dark, and thought he heard something? Thought he saw something? And emptied his M-1 (from about twenty feet away) in the direction of what he thought was the enemy. My poncho was not his enemy! He killed it anyway; six of the eight rounds he fired punched holes in it. Ruined the damn thing, I took his.

He turned out to be a good guy to have around in a pinch, it takes a little time. Combat is a nightmare at first and much worse at night. The mind can play tricks in the dark of night, fear can twist what isn't into what is, sounds sneak up, shadows move and become reality. Green troops are at the mercy of their demons in the first few dark nights of combat, especially untrained Troops.

Some days or weeks later my squad was on patrol and unknown to us two half-tracts with quad-fifties opened up on a hill ahead of us, their fire going low over our heads, needless to say everyone hit the dirt real fast. Only an Infantryman can go from the standing position to being a half an inch thick on the ground in the wink of an eye. We thought "ambush" and I rolled to a depression pulled the pin from a grenade while desperately looking for the machine gun position to lob it at. There wasn't one, I was left holding a grenade with no pin and feeling a bit foolish. Had there been any movement in the bushes, at that time under those conditions, I would

194

have instinctively thrown the grenade and had to live with my mistake had they been refugees.

Throw green troops into battle without adequate training, no communication equipment, no interpreter, get hit with our own air strike with refugees all around, and the stage will be set for total confusion. Guerrilla activity was a fact of life in those days and they did slip through our lines with the refugees. Rumors would have run rampant about everything, North Koreans mixed with refugees, orders not true, orders that were true, the captain said kill them all! He told you that? No, I heard it from someone. They would have heard orders that were lawful, rumors that were unlawful the chain of command was broken. The whole North Korean army was about to be on top of them. Troops were spread out to thin for the senior non-coms and officers to have the control over the series of events about to unfold.

Lets set the stage as I see it at "No Gun Ri";

Green troops land at Pohangdong and two days later they are in the area of the enemy (in reality there was no front line, they were segments of lines). They would have heard the stories and rumors of Suwan and Tajion and be expecting the worse.

Not furnishing ROK interpreters were a terrible injustice to the troops and the civilians, blame the Generals in Tokyo.

Being strafed by our own aircraft, which very well could have mistaken our troops mixed in with the refugees as the enemy, adding to the confusion. Some of our own men took cover under the railroad bridge to escape the strafing and our riflemen opened up on them along with the refugees.

Panic, confusion and orders/rumors too vague were passed down the chain of command. i.e. don't let any refugees thru our lines. How do you stop thousands of refugees from coming thru? (There were over five million refugees in the Korean War and much of their migrations occurred in the first few months) Fire on them but use discretion where it involves women and children??? What the hell is that supposed to mean? Enemy disguised as refugees! How does one discern foe from innocent??? What does one do? When does one do it? Where is the lieutenant? Can't let them out from under the Railroad Bridge, by now they are sure there are enemy in with them.

Machine gun positions would have been on each side of the railroad tracks so there would be a field of fire on each side that is normal. (Korean survivor claims the machine firing into the tunnel would begin after darkness set in, this is vital to my claim this was not a massacre.)

The probable Scenario

Darkness falls and the ghosts of death began to stir in the green troops, far off sounds seem close and the dark reveals shifting shapes, which were there only in the minds of ill trained and ill led young boys. One rifleman or machine gunner panics and fires at one of these damn imagined movements or sounds, the whole area erupts in gunfire directed at the culvert where they believe the enemy is. As the tracers ricochet thru the culvert the ones on the other side believe they are under attack from the culvert and return the fire that ricochet thru into our troops on the other side. Now troops on each side of the culverts know the enemy is in the culverts. So goes the battle. So goes mixed up confusion. So goes the lives of innocents and so goes an unintended massacre by green, under trained, confused and frightened American boys.

Had this been an ordered massacre the refugees would have been all killed in a short period of time, it doesn't take (three nights?) to kill a few hundred trapped inside a culvert. According to one Korean survivor we helped bury some dead the next morning and gave medical care to the survivors. Does this sound like a planned massacre? Only someone with no concept of the situation would say yes. American boys will/would carry the pain of this time with them unto the grave, only death will relieve the guilt and pain, which is quite sad.

The investigative reporters did not go far enough, they went just far enough to meet their agenda (of attempting) to disgrace the values of the Korean War Veterans and the honour of some green troops of long ago. Nay, worse yet they would bring disgrace on all who fought in Korea and in the minds of many Americans their agenda will be met, the vast and continued coverage by the press and media will assure it.

jimmie joe

There will be no Pulitzer Prize for trash writings that leave out pertinent facts and have no competency to evaluate, that which is truth.

P.S. I was wrong, the incompetent Asses were awarded it.

The finding by the U.S. and Korean Government investigation agreed with what I wrote in 1999, a massacre by Panicked green troops lacking adequately trained Officers and Non-coms. Reporters who knew nothing about green troops, combat confusion and night time, would read the exact information this report was based on and come to a conclusion one hundred eighty degrees different.

The reporters wanted the incident to be a coldly calculated massacre so they slanted the investigation in that direction, this was quite easy to do after fifty years. The reporters worked around a bit of truth and gleaned a Pulitzer Prize, the object of the investigation from the first.

jim woods

Flower Children from Vietnam to Kosovo

May, 2001KOSOVO

It's something needs asking my friends;

What reasoning does Congress use to come up with the excuse, as they vote in favor of a resolution backing the president, *they cannot let our fighting men down?* Either the cause was justified or it was not. How many of you damn congressmen recall the Gulf of Tonkin Lie? Body bags held nearly sixty thousand men you didn't let down. What does "can't let the Troops down" mean to you? Did you donate to their BLACK MARBLE WALL? Yes, Congress you alone made possible the donation of Dead young Boys names. You could have stopped the Vietnam War anytime in those years. It is your sacred duty to question our "cause" in a war, Korea and Vietnam lasted much to long, and you failed our living and our dead.

In the Korean War the last twenty-six months were spent taking, losing, retaking the same hills and ridges over and over. The battle lines moved very little after July of nineteen fifty-one from where they were at the Armistice but the fighting and killing remained. Somehow our Country let us down in Korea, before, during and after the battles ended. For over Two years Congress left young Men dying on hills and ridges for no gain, for absolutely nothing, because they did absolutely nothing to stop it.

Congress let the Vietnam War continue for ten years after the Gulf of Tonkin, it took an eruption of Civilians against the War before Congress would intercede, all those dead young Men, all the dead Vietnamese numbering in millions. Congress's shame not the Grunts.

The president should never be allowed the kind of power to commit our country to war. Congress must get the gonads to rule by our Constitution. The way congress lets us down is by sending our young people to die in an unjust cause or when they allow our missiles and bombs to kill the innocent. Only our enemies are war criminals?

Even tho I wrote the poem, which follows this dissertation, I had decided not to publish. I had mostly come to terms with the thought, maybe, just maybe, the ones who ran and the young who protested the war in Vietnam did so out of true caring about the civilians being killed and the deceptiveness and/or righteousness of the cause.

With the war in Serbia (A small country the size of Ohio) I must reconsider which I had nearly come to accept.

You flower children of the mid-sixties to the mid-seventies are nowhere to be found thirty years later with our massive bombing in Yugoslavia, why is this?

1 — You're way past Draft age?
2 — There is no Draft?
3 — It's not the" in thing" anymore?
4 — War and killing of the innocent is now acceptable since you've matured?

You stopped one War that badly needed stopping and claimed your reasons were Honourable. The results were Honourable, I'm not sure about your hearts. (Your treatment of our returning Veterans had no honour), How much did you "flower children" contribute to their inability to adjust and how many suicides, which still go on, have you "compassionate flower children" caused thru your actions of around thirty years ago?

We have flown about thirty thousand sorties at altitudes above twelve to fifteen thousand feet so as not to lose aircraft. This is not normal to a pilot when attacking troops or a convoy. The target (with the angle of attack) can't be identified from four miles away. So we have Civilians trying to flee the war zone being killed.

We have been strafed by our own aircraft, the pilots couldn't identify us from about one half mile away. To begin firing four miles away from target of unknown humans is a political tactic! It is wrong. It is criminal.

NATO has lost no pilots but a hell of a lot of innocents have died because of political pressure not to lose pilots, the hell with civilians lives lost thru not being able to identify innocent from foe. Laws of land warfare are now antiquated.

There is no question these tactics are something our pilots should (hopefully) hate, being aware it is wrong to put the innocent at risk when this can be mostly avoided by closer observation of the targets.

A well thought plan by our commander-in-chief. (Stay high—Don't die) ** Hell man, I fought a war and killed about??? Thousand humans and never lost a man! What a guy! Could we have used Willie in Vietnam leading a line platoon? ** He could have been, he should have been. He should have seen the horror decisions made ten thousand miles away cause. Let him feel their pain, let him taste their fear, let him view the dead and dying Children and let him live with it for his lifetime.

Any excuse will be willingly accepted by a booming economy, any spin the Oval Office wishes to use will by faithfully reported by you of Americas fourth estate with no investigative reporting, no probing questions and no honour for your profession. It's all right if Clinton and Albright piss on your pant leg while spinning. You are clones of liberal professors to whom truth is irrelevant and honour is a misspelled word.

Collateral damage is such a sterile word, which for some reason is accepted as not a very big deal and a necessary part of war. The greater questions are; is the war necessary? Or where the hell have the brilliant diplomats and State Department been in the years preceding a decision to go to war? And where is/was Congress, why, I sometimes wonder, the hell do we have a Constitution?

Who made the decision to use cluster bombs at random on the wooded areas? They couldn't find the enemy in the open and decided they must be hiding in the woods, lets bomb the crap out of the woods, the hell with the civilians who were also hiding in the woods to get away from the Serbs and the bombing of the cities. Some questions should be asked about the whole conduct of NATO and our political leaders.

Any questions Flower Children? I thought not. You don't hear what I hear or see what I see. I hear the sound of bombers in the night, I see Mothers huddled with their Children in a cold dark basement, their frightened eyes looking up thru the dark ceiling when they hear the sound of jets, Mama pulls them close and says it will be all right. I feel fear you can cut with a knife in the Mothers heart, fear her Children won't live to see the sunrise tomorrow, or the day after, or the day after that. She must live thru seventy-eight nights of terror wondering each night if her Children will see that special sunrise, the one bringing peace and no death from the sky.

Did you hear the bombers flower children? Did you feel the concussion shake the house from a nearby hit? Did you feel the Mothers fear? Did you feel the Children's fear in that cold dank basement? We were wrong in our approach and method of solving a problem that has existed in the Balkans for centuries. We kill thousands of innocents rather than assassinate one man and there are no outcries from the old flower children of nearly forty years ago. May God forgive us!

Tell me were you flower children ever really real?

PS: You are of course aware of bombs we tested filled with some kind of carbon fiber that temporarily shut down all the power in Belgrade, it worked quite well. It temporally shut down all the little Babies incubators and all life support machines of others.

It permanently shut down the little babies along with others. Why would we even consider such a ———— ———— I am very much afraid we have become or are close to becoming the type of people and nation we use to go to war to fight. Still no outrage from our safe, aging, balding, gray-haired, paunchy bellied flower children. ———— Go figure!

Ethnic cleansing is the lowest of the low in any country's conduct against Humanity.

Damn the worlds politicians, the safe, fat, contemptuous, flag waving bastards who consider a crime against Humanity as something only the loser can commit and be prosecuted for. The egotistical asses never even consider that "war itself is a crime against Humanity".

On the other side of this coin is a statement that is equally true, but the cases are more rare than the world seems to believe. "A crime against Humanity" is abstention from intervening and preventing "Crimes against Humanity" by the power of governments against their own peoples.

We generally have not reached this stage of civilized wisdom to discern the timely intervention into the internal affairs of another country. World politics must, and it is critical they do, play a large part in any decision of intervention.

The collective wisdom of the world's leaders must evolve far beyond its present degree if we are to be free of pure politics in our evaluation, than prevention, of the continued massacring of a people within a sovereign nation by said sovereign nation.

I agree the massacring of a nations own citizens is a cause for intervention, however the scales must be balanced with fairness of that which has actually occurred without using political rhetoric as proof or innocence in deciding a massacre is or is not a reality. Whether the time has come for some legally commissioned force to intervene, and the methods of warring we will use to stop it is where wisdom is paramount.

Many countries, including some members of NATO considered our conduct against Serbia to be acts of war crimes.

Because America, with or without NATO, is extremely powerful we must accept the fact power does not give us wisdom. Power does not give us special rights we would deny other countries and power in the tactics we use in our conduct of warfare will not assuage our culpability of the innocent deaths we cause.

Very few hard facts were presented by any media source on Kosovo and Serbia prior to our intervention. Due to the massive amount of propaganda spewed forth from the Clinton administration, immediately after we began the bombing, I must question the basic premise of not only the legality but also the timing and it's validity.

For several years the Albanian Liberation forces had made forays into Kosovo attacking police stations, assassinating mayors, sometime their families, and various other public officials. [We must remember Serbia and Kosovo are what is left of Yugoslavia; they are the same sovereign country.] This went on for years and was to that degree covered on slow news days by the media, I can recall very little coverage of the Serbians committing mass killings of Albanians in Kosovo prior to Clintons committing our air war. Earlier in Bosnia, Croatia, and other areas of the Balkans all of the countries were engaged in ethnic cleansing with mass executions of innocent defenseless peoples and Serbia was probably the guiltiest.

Former Yugoslav President Slobodan Milosevic was and is a murderous bastard who must face the court at The Hague; there are many others in the Balkans including the Albanian terrorists who have been equally as guilty of crimes against Humanity. In my mind NATO also must answer for their methods of solving the Kosovo/Serbian crises.

Macedonia is now, in 2001, the country facing the problem of Albanian Liberation forces to impose their demands using methods much the same as those that were successful in Kosovo. When Macedonia attempts to squash this Guerrilla type warfare will NATO again step in on the side of the terrorists?

We send our Warriors into harms way in the Balkans while at the same time many nations in Africa are committing mass ethnic cleansing to a much greater degree. Slavery along with ethnic cleansing against the Christians by the Muslims in the Sudan has been and still is taking place. The media gives very little coverage to most horrors taking place in Africa; I'll let you ascertain the reason.

From; "Little, Children—Grown-ups War"
Page 54
Ask about the little Children,
the ones you will never see.
The unnumbered maimed and dying Children,
the ones so far from you or me.

Some of them are Chinks you know,
or Japs, Ragheads or Gooks.
There's Niggers there in Africa
and Spearchuckers and Spooks.

There's Infidels and Sloops and Kikes
and names not known by me.
Worlds' drums of war will always claim
they're subhuman enemies.

The above lines are from a poem about little Children dying in the Korea war where millions of innocent lives were lost. Causing the deaths of any helpless Humans, Men, Women or Children is deplorable, dead innocent adults only seem less appalling in our minds than the death of Children. Our innocent casualties of war, be they maimed or killed, have no age that changes anything.

Jimmie joe
Fishhook junction, alaska

The runners

Following will be some rhymes of how I felt about those who dodged the draft for reasons that were not acceptable by law. The ones who ran to another country rather than face going to war or prison are my main theme. I don't feel as strongly about them now but somehow there is still a bit of disdain for such as they.

I commend those who protested against the war by directing their anger toward the politicians, as this was the correct procedure. I also commend the students at the democratic convention in Chicago in 1968. I certainly question where you were during the seventy-eight days we were dropping bombs on Serbia and Kosovo.

Those who took their displaced anger out on our troops did a very deep disservice to these men, totally unjust and unfair. They caused immeasurable damage to minds already numb and coping with horrors most of us will never have to face, that damage still's there to this day for many of these men.

I offer no apology for the way I feel about draft dodging Runners who could have made a statement by choosing prison. Those who spat on and jeered our troops returning from combat I hold in unspeakable contempt.

You're country called, to war you went.
A dodger now is president.

The Runners

Politically correct I will not be,
I refuse to stoop so low.
I'm going to rhyme the way I feel
about the ones who wouldn't go.

You who ran to Canada
there's more I have to say,
I know you objected to that war,
your reasons do not play.

You claim you made a statement
'bout our war in Vietnam.
You claim you made a statement.
I don't give a damn.
"william jefferson clinton" man.

You had a chance to do your part
as a medic without a gun.
You had no courage, a cowards heart,
to save yourself you run.

No courage for the prison,
no courage for the war.
Just somewhere for your safety,
from self could expect no more.

Now if you'd went to prison
I'd think you had some guts,
instead you ran away and hid,
I know you have no nuts.

You should have filled our prisons
with true objecting men.
Then your cause would have risen,
they'd have listened to you then.

You picked the safe and easy way,
your morals were not true.
Your cause in truth does not play
from runners such as you.

Those who took their prison term,
some respect those men did earn.
I respect the men that served much more,
especially the Infantry in war.

Your safety's why you left this land,
escape the prison or the war.
The thought of Bubba you can't stand,
the thought of dying you abhor.

Other men can take your place
with Bubba or the dying.
Did you spit in the Veterans face?
or thank the Vet for trying?

There's a price we pay for freedom,
there's a price that honour pays.
A patriot must pay the price.
A coward runs away.

Men of courage answer call,
men of honour take the chance.
Runners? Cowards piss in Cowards pants.

All these acts you could amend,
at least to some degree.
You owe our homeless Veteran men.
They kept you runners free.

You know someone took your place,
did he come home in body bag?
Men like you feel no disgrace?
Your conscience feels no nag?

You had your choice of prison,
you had your choice of war.
Either one is honour,
they show what men stand for.

I think you stand for nothing
but I'm rhyming this for me.
A bit of my old anger,
my old anger to set free.
Direct to you from me.

jimmie joe

jimmie joe

slick willies dictionary

According to draft dodging bill
which he stated on TV
You can't hate your government
and still love your country.

I truly swear I'm one that cares
and love my country well.
I truly state I've come to hate
our government from hell.

Politicians lies I loathe, despise,
lack of honor I disdain.
Draft dodging bill there on the hill
causes my soul deep pain.

He's not the first, he is the worse
and him I quite despise.
Dishonor flows as his nose grows
from deceit and his damn lies.

I really dislike the draft dodging tike
but serious I can't be.
This non-sex pun is too much fun,
I'll type it just for me and
include it here for thee.

I have to say he might be okay
if his thoughts on sex are true.
Perhaps in his mind you will not find
a thought that he will rue.

Draft dodging bill just dodged the draft,
this might be his only wrong.
If I think this way I must be daft
or inhaling on my bong.

Draft dodging bill kinda gets a thrill
from ladies young and fair.
In our White House he'll have a joust
with sweet young interns there.

Liberals will say this is okay
draft dodging bill's our man.
He needs relief, it's his belief
it's better than his hand

If I am caught, doing sex that's naught
with my buddy's' sweet young wife.
She did to me, not me to she,
my buddy won't feel strife?

I'll have my fun, I'm number one,
she has sooo much to give.
Buddy don't feel grief? I need relief.
Do you think he'll let me live?

It must cause strife to bills' poor wife
to raise a kid like bill.
It wasn't sex, that girl's a hex,
she's a slick willie thrill.

I was a fool, behind a one room school
I was ignorant as could be.
These little games, we played with dames
sure felt like sex too me.

Webster's a shame, he has no name
for this fun that isn't sex.
We'll have to fake, a name we'll make,
perhaps we'll call it Rex!!

Rex won't do? it's up to you,
it has to have a name.
Cause we'll rue the day when we can't play
this feel good little game.

We can't play a game that has no name,
we just won't know how to ask.
It's kind of rough, making names is tough,
it's not a easy task.

Draft dodging bill there on the hill
complicates my life.
I ask my friend, what's this portend?
I even ask his wife.

My friend don't know, something 'bout blow,
his wife just smiled a bit.
This is insane, we need a name
but I can't think of it.

.We could call it wow!! or holy cow!!
or even call it bill.
We could call it aaahh!! or ummpapa!!
or a simple name like thrill.

We'll call it unzip or thrust your hip!!
that would be all right.
We could call it sleaze or on your knees!!
or oval room at night.

Bill can't control his lust so bold,
cause Billy needs relief.
That damn blue dress, an awful mess,
his aim's beyond belief.

Billy you fool, unhand that tool
or trouble will drop by.
That blue dress will hang your roving wang
and catch you in your lie.

Bill don't understand, hell he's a man
and has his manly needs,
There's lots a smut when Bill's in rut
and sows his manly seeds.

I'm off the track, I must get back
to finding that damn name.
We could call it joy!! or just ooh boy!!
or a blowing bubbles game!!!.

We could call it please or don't you sneeze!!
or maybe call it just say aaah.
We could call it dine or trim my vine,
but I still like ummpapa!!

.We could call it pop pop
or try fizz fizz
or "O" what a relief it is.

If I could spell I'd name it well,
a name perhaps "endorphin".
This is no joke, it'll replace coke
and there will be no abortion.

We could call it Ted, no! mr. Ed!!
that's the name I've found.
Me and my hun we'll have some fun,
great fun this horsing around.

211

No that's kinda crude and I'm not rude,
with this naming I am done.
I'm telling you that I am thru,
I'll just call it "lotsafun!!"

jimmie joe,
fishhook junction, alaska

justa bit of jimmie's wit

Swear'n,Ly'n Kid—On the farm

When I was just a little Lad,
I weren't so good and I weren't so bad.
I were kinda somewhere inbetween,
most times Ia's kind, sometimes Ia's mean.

It t'weren't honorable to lie,
I was brung up that way.
Sometimes I'd slip and then the whip
ud make me rue the day.

T'weren't no time outs with lies about,
no to your room be sent.
The whip was there, bend over chair.
on bare heinie rage was vent.

They'd say yaa shor this'll hurt me more
than it's gonna hurt you.
As that whip sliced air toward me butt bare
I knew that just t'weren't true.

I will be good, I screamed I would,
would I lie anymore?
No! No! I'd yell, it hurt s like hell.
OOPS; the whip begins galore.

I'm nearly dead, me butt's beet red,
the tears begin to flow.
I'm really sad that I've been bad,
please Ma let that whip go.

In pain I'm mired but her arm's tired,
I can see she's almost done.
They make real hurts those riding quirts,
lyin sure just hain't much fun.

I'll lie no more 'cause I done swore
me lyin days has ended.
I'll stand for meals 'til red butt heals
and "GOD"'s no more offended.

A promise made's not a debt unpaid
to a lyin kid like me.
If I could escape troubles I make
than a lyin kid I'd be.

Some time I won and 'twas good fun
to beat Ma with me lyin.
Still 'twas for naught when I got caught
and me butt felt it 'twere fryin.

I'd get in dutch not very much,
just oncest a week or so.
I shoulda learned 'cause me butt burned.
Dumb lyin kids are slow!

Parents don't like their little tikes
say'n bad words right out loud.
We'd sneak away and the words we'd say'd
make fourteen sailors proud.

We'd swear at stones and dead horse bones
and the air 'twould just turn blue.
Webster'd be proud and rave out loud
at the words that we went thru.

From our hay mow we'd swear at cows,
I think it made 'um sad.
They'd just say moo, that's all they'd do,
sure 'twas fun being bad.

When I'd cuss at Jack, He'd cuss right back,
we 'twas some real fun guys.
We'd swear at trees and bumble bees
and at phallic clouds in sky.

We'd cuss at stumps and plow horse rumps,
we hit everything in view.
We'd never swear if adults 'twas there.
That's a dumb thing to do.

I'm in a fret, where did we get
those cuss words in our heads?
Not from our Pa, sure not from Ma,
that doggone uncle Ted?

Can't remember where, but words 'twas there
and some were mighty fine.
Each cuss word they said stuck in our head,
most are too bad to rhyme.

We'd peek at girls with pretty curls
and try to catch 'em bare.
"twas tough to do, but a time or two
we did and did we stare!

There's sumtin wrong, they got no d-ng!
I'd better run and MaMa tell.
Jack kinda smart, called me dumb f-rt,
Said she'd whup me all to hell.

215

Jack tried to 'splain, I got no brain,
it kinda worried me.
Without no d-ng lots can go wrong,
just how can girls go p?

I'm glad I'm a boy, I got this toy,
I can p near forty feet.
Your name I'll write in snow pure white.
Don't cha think that's neat?

Girls hain't no fun when boys are young
they always tell on you.
They run to Ma, sometimes to Pa
we'd lie and say, not true!

Pa, we didn't swear at that cow there,
not at that dumb stupid cow.
I swore at that one by the door.
Oh, oh in trouble agin now.

Bend this young fool over milkin stool.
Me mouth did it agin.
It's butt beet red then off to bed.
Swearing 'n lyin's a bad sin

I caught a big snake down by the lake
hid it in me sister's room.
T'was real great fun, see 'em scream 'n run,
Ma tryin to kill it with a broom.

She broke kerosene lamp, didn't get the scamp
broke dishes everywhere.
Took lotsa swings, couldn't get the thing.
Shoulda heard me mad ma swear

I couldn't believe, ears must deceive,
those words me ma don't spout.
With every swing cuss words would ring
and echo miles about.

Musta been a curse, cause times got worse
as she struck a mighty blow.
Missed that big snake, hit sister Kate,
'twas a fine blow don't ch'know.

I tell ya it's true, me sister flew
'bout clean across that room.
Broke Granpa's chair 'n just laid there,
Ma swung a real mean broom.

I figgered I'd step in and stop this din,
I reached down and grabbed that snake.
Believe me you 'twern't the thing to do
'cause Ma's brain came wide awake.

Her eyes caught mine and a light did shine,
not a pleasant sight to see.
They glowed bright red, I thought, I'm dead
or real soon I'm gonna be.

I was almost right, I took off in flight,
that broom Ma couldn't ride.
I'm here to tell she tried like hell.
It gave me time to hide.

I figgered I'll stay here for forty years
and with Moses I'd camp out.
I'll come to harm back on the farm
with that screaming witch about.

It gave me a chill, me blood she'll spill
if she gets her claws on me.
When she learns to fly her broom in sky
A dead kid thru life I'll be.

I hate that snake from by the lake,
Look how he caused me pain.
It's his fault I know, that I can't show
Me face at home again.

I'll make him dead, I'll smash his head
and that'll fix him good.
I'll take him to Pa and he'll tell Ma,
Pa always understood.

It didn't work, Ma grabbed that quirt
near before that I walked in.
Dad grabbed me hair, made me butt bare,
Ma's eyes turned red like sin.

Big horns she grew, a forked tail too,
What happened to me Ma?
She looked evil mean, 'taint Halloween,
Ya gotta help me Pa!

Pa said now hon, he's our only son
And he didn't mean no hurt.
Ma didn't care, 'twas over chair
and that devil's riding quirt.

Pa let her go for an hour or so,
at least it seemed to me.
Her horns fell off and her mouth lost froth,
she turned back to me mommie.

.I got over that and courage grew fat
in about a week or two.
I did my chores and played outdoors,
I was goody two shoes.

Life t'wern't no fun being perfect son,
I was bored like that dead snake.
There's neighbor girls with pretty curls
who naughty pleasures make.

'Twas best fun to swear but I declare
girls kinda changed me view,
Thought it was dumb, couldn't be no fun
what they wanted me to do.

A lot I knew, I'm telling you
'Twas fun as it could be!
Sure made me glow there down below,
a good naughty game for me.

I was too young and not yet -ung
but lower region glowed, Oh boy!
This bran new game without no name
kinda pleased me p'n toy.

Never got caught doin sex that's naught,
I was too young anyway.
Girls lied like hell, they tried to tell
'tis a game our parents play.

It made me mad 'cause mom and dad
Wouldn't play that naughty game.
I don't know why those girls would lie,
dumb girls hain't got no brain.

In twelve years more, I'll quite adore
the women my heart will hold.
The love will stay, won't go away
thru life as I grow old.

That's 'nough that kinda stuff,
back to pre-puberty.
Me younger times I put in rhymes
A swearin ly'n kid I be.

I copped a cigar from Pa's old car,
thought I'd have meself a smoke.
I came to harm behind the barn,
smokin's a pukin' joke.

Me chest puffed out, I looked about,
no one else was there,
felt real grownup as I lit up
and sucked in smoke filled air.

I'm tellin you, t'weren't thing to do,
it durn near strangled me.
Me lungs don't care for smoke filled air,
a wimp is what I be.

This dumb ly'n kid, know what he did?
Took another puff or two
Or three or four or maybe more,
boy, what I put me thru.

Me stomach churned, my throat sure burned,
the world spun like a top.
Me gills turned green, pukin's obscene
but damn, I couldn't stop.

Me breakfast went as tummy rent
it out upon the ground.
Yesterday's lunch and last month's brunch
was splattered all around.

Cows kinda stared and at me glared
'bout the mess I'd made on grass,
that dumb kid, look what he did
lyin, stupid swearin'—s.

I couldn't stand on rolling land,
I reeled like a drunkin bum.
I couldn't walk, I couldn't talk,
this smokin hain't no fun.

I've had enough, I hain't as tough
as Dad or Uncle Ted.
Cigars is bad, they make me sad
and almost make me dead.

Havin bare feet hain't very neat
in hay fields newly mown.
The stubble there would make us swear
'n walk funny, jump 'n groan.

Stubble's not neat on tender feet
in early summer days.
Walkin's rough when feet hain't tough
but it helps your swearin ways.

Shoes t'wern't about when school let out
'cause money just t'wern't there.
We'd hobble round on hurtin ground
and try to walk on air.

One sunny day while puttin up hay
Uncle Ted gave me a chaw.
Red man was sweet, 'twas fun to eat,
put grown-up lump in jaw.

In a short while, I lost me smile,
me gut it kinda rolled.
Uncle Ted just grinned; he's devil's kin,
I'll die 'fore I git old.

'Taint very neat what adults eat,
it makes for a pukin' lad.
It gives um joy to make a boy
just puke and feel quite bad.

A glass of wine would be just fine
for a ly'n kid like me.
A great big glass kinda kicked me—s
and filled Uncle John with glee.

Barf time agin, it made em grin
at this kid they made so sick.
It don't seem right, their pure delight
in playin pukin' trick.

I'm here to tell they grin like hell
when kids get kinda green.
Just hain't no reason for open season
on little kids, that's mean.

Haint no fun bein stupid one
'n the men just laugh at you,
Just hain't fair, but they don't care
'bout pain they put boys thru.

The girls so sweet they didn't treat
the way they treated boys,
they didn't swear if girls 'twas there
or treat them to pukin' joys.

I thank you folks who played the jokes
on us boys back on the farm.
Looking back was fun being kinda dumb,
good memories, no harm.

jimmie joe
fishhook junction, alaska

Dragon Poop

When Granny'd scold of Hell she told,
sure scared it out of me.
Brimstone burned and Sulfur churned
and you couldn't breathe or see.

You'd go there if by chance you'd swear
or do most anything.
The coals red hot would hurt a lot
inside that fire ring.

In God you trust, believe you must
and say your Prayers at night.
If you do wrong Boy you are Gone!
She gave an awful fright.

The Devil needs young Boys to feed
her hungry Dragons there.
It takes a week for them to Eat
one small bad Boy baked rare.

The Devil she dances with glee
when she sees him so forlorn.
He's kind of fat, Dragons like that.
They're glad that he'd been born.

Fat bad Boys are Dragons joys,
Dragons think they taste real fine.
As you they munch, your bones will crunch
and your guts they feed to swine.

As they chew on you they'll slurp blood too
a grinning all the while.
The Devil she will be happy
and wear a Devils toothy smile.

When the week is thru, they're done with you,
but there still is more to tell.
This part is sad, if you've been bad
it'll make you scream and yell.

When they are thru I assure you
of a nasty awful fact,
you're Dragon Poop, they use a scoop
and to life they bring you back!

Again you're a Boy and no ones joy
'cause you're made of Dragon Poop.
The dragons wish to make a dish
they use you for Poop soup.

(Between you and me this shouldn't be
but Granny say's it's so.
I'm just a Kid, but after what I did
my Granny ought to know.)

When they are thru what's left of you
they poop out on the floor.
Here comes the scoop for Dragon Poop
and you're a sh-tty Kid once more

jimmie joe

"My Dad"

When I was a little lad 'bout three
a brand new Father came to me
The face of old one I didn't know,
he'd left Mom about two years ago.

New Dad bounced me on his knee,
held my finger, walked with me.
Worked for fifty cents a day,
a bad depression's under way.

Had to feed four kids and Mom,
quite a chore my Dad took on.
Worked all day on farm next door,
came home, Dad had to work some more.

I never knew Dad to get mad,
I had myself a real fine Dad.
If I was allowed my Dad to pick,
I'd pick this Dad, I'd pick him quick.

I never knew my Dad to swear,
at least I can't recall.
Never knew Dad to drink a beer
or take a drink at all.

My Dad always treated people kind,
I never knew Dad to be mean.
My Dad he was a gentle man,
the finest Dad I've seen.

I was an average boy I guess
into my teenage tour,
Kind of forgot my Dad was best
until my brain got more mature.

I joined the army at eighteen,
training camp was far away.
Memory slipped 'bout my fine Dad
but for me he still did pray.

We never fought or anything,
life then was filled with fun.
It was my time to try my wings,
my Dad knew I was still his son.

Went overseas, foxholes are bad,
there's things I've left unsaid.
God, one more time let me see my Dad
to give thanks from his loving son.

Thanks for taking care of Mom
and my three Sisters too.
I'm lucky that I had you there,
pray God I turn out like you.

I came home from battle time,
furlough at home I can't recall.
I'm sure My Dad, sure Dad helped me
Like Dad always helped us all.

All thru our lives we got along,
like Father, Son and Friend.
In Florida I'd visit Dad,
didn't get there at the end.

Fourteenth of December of 1990
in his Chrysler car Dad died.
He was t-boned by a speeding car,
.it struck the drivers side.

Dad felt no pain and I believe
Dad and Mom are playing up above.
I'm thankful for the times I my told Dad
I had a Dad like him to love.

I love you Dad and miss you too
and I'll see you in a while.
I again thank God for a Dad like you.
Heaven gained by Daddies smile.

When I pass thru my veil of life
to your land beyond the sky,
I'll have your hand to help me thru
for what fate awaits me when I die.

I walk in peace, thanks Dad to you.
Thank you Dad, *I Love you, jim*

Dad and Mom visited me in Alaska in nineteen-seventy two, the same year they both retired, it was the last time I saw Mom alive. I should have taken a trip outside to visit but I had my hands full raising my Children. I should have found a way as nine years later in nineteen eighty-one Mom died of a heart attack.

Many of us tend to assume our parents are going to live forever, time passes and catches up quite fast and we're left with "I should haves". I did visit Dad in Florida for a few months at a time in the years 1984, 85 and 89.

Dad was eighty years old when he was killed and in reasonably good health, his Mother lived to be ninety-eight and his Grandmother died at one hundred and eight. Dad could have had a few more years.

I am aware Dad had a huge impact on my life. I miss him. I love him. He was the most honourable man I have ever met.

Dad I'm proud to be Your Son, Jim

Baby jimmy joe

Date of birth, June 21, 1954,

This is my ode to jimmy joe,
it's very hard to write.
I know in sadness tears will flow,
to me now it's all right.

Twenty-first of June, nineteen fifty-four
my first born Son was given,
I could not ask for to much more,
'twas a special gift from Heaven.

Big blue eyes and lots of hair
and chubby cheeks had he.
I'd hold him crooked in my left arm
and his eyes would lock with me.

Those big blue eyes stared into mine
and caused my heart to glow.
These feelings are hard to express.
Thank God I loved him so.

I pray jimmy felt that Love that flowed
to his soul from eyes of dad.
I pray little jimmies small heart glowed
as way back then mine had.

Jimmies time on earth was much to short,
so little time for joy.
I pray jimmy felt dads Love for him.
My little Baby, my Baby Boy.

Date of death, August 27, 1954

I awoke early one morning
and tears flowed, I knew not why.
Some precious(???) was missing.
Tears flowed.—I didn't cry.

Little jimmy touched me in my sleep,
jimmy came to say good-bye.
I can't explain, when I awoke
I knew jimmy joe had died.

On little jimmies birthday
every year since then.
I'd wonder what he'd look like
and figure how old he'd been.

I still remember big blue eyes
not wavering from mine,
I still remember how I felt
even after all this time.

Thank you little jimmy joe
for the time you spent with me.
Thanks for making my heart glow,
thanks for those memories.

After my Helen passed away,
'specially after all my rhymes,
I'd ask her to look after you,
guess dads kind of dumb at times.

I don't remember you in death,
my mind that did not keep.
I do remember Loving you.
Good-bye my Son. — I weep.

It's all right Son I Love you,
I know you understand.
I feel you're still a Baby,
but you might be a man.

I know you are an Angel,
waiting in Angel land.
Please pray for me my jimmy
and someday take my hand.
I love you, daddy

The Alaska Flag Song

Eight stars of gold on a field of blue,
Alaska's flag, may it mean to you,
The blue of the sea, the evening sky.
The mountain lakes and the flowers nearby.

The gold of the early sourdough's dream,
The precious gold of the hills and streams,
The brilliant star in the northern ski,
The Bear, the Dipper, and shining high,

The Great North Star with a steady light,
O'er land and sea, a beacon, bright.
Alaska's Flag. to Alaskan's dear,
The simple flag of a Last Frontier.

Little jimmie didn't get to see my Alaska, maybe he is seeing it thru me, and I hope so because the last forty years have been grand. I hope he has felt my contentment while fishing in all the wild places of Alaska.

I hope he felt my fear tracking a bear at night with a flashlight, a bear I had wounded just before dark, I hope he felt my shame for not making a better shot.

231

I hope little Jimmie felt my throat go dry with fear as Rip tides tossed my boat around for hours, in sunshine then fog, as I slowly made headway around Gore Point to the safety of the sheltered cove at Portlock, Alaska.

The following are some odds and ends from when I began to fumble my way thru to find the beginning, some love, some anger, some hate and some pain and as far as love goes a lot of missing, wanting and maybe not needing, but boy it sure would be nice.

A bit of one fingered typing as I was just learning. I'm still mostly one fingered, the only difference is I'm faster and I use the upper case occasionally and I do sneak in an extra finger now and then.

This erratic search thru my mind, for who the hell knows what, may very well be boring to most readers. I included these rhymes of search as a stimulant for readers with extremely boring lives.

"My Helen"

back in may of nineteen-fifty
the army made a decision.
lets transfer corporal jimmie joe
to the twenty-fourth division.

that idea was fine with me
I couldn't wait to go.
I'd never crossed the wide, wide sea,
but first a home furlough.

for thirty days I'll have some fun
and all that sort of thing.
by chasing girls in summers sun
to make this lads heart ring.

I met one thru my cousin jack,
her face I could adore.
she made my heart flip off its track,
had not been done before.

when our eyes met we couldn't pry
our eyes apart — they're stuck.
we didn't even want to try.
can cupid run amok?

heaven must be a lot like this
I really hope that's so.
somehow we had an instant bliss,
our eyes did glow, they let us know.

I reached and took her hands in mine
them softly I did hold.
our probing eyes sought out divine
as we viewed each others soul.

cousin jack he kind of stared,
then looked at clouds in sky.
I nor Helen really cared
lost in each others eyes.

we forgot he was around,
did not mean to be rude.
our limpid eyes they did astound
our feelings and our mood.
both of us just standing there.
just holding hands; just holding stare.

didn't know then about cupids charms,
I was a bit naive.
quite soon I'll hold her in my arms
and boy will I believe!

almost our eyes seemed to reveal,
a knowing back thru time.
almost a love, was almost real.
soul mate with hand in mine.

some past life could it be?
is there maybe such a thing?
Helen was holding hands with me
and thru time our hearts did sing?

somehow I mumbled (hard to speak)
I was confused you see.
felt real goofy, my knees were weak,
just didn't seem like me.

it didn't make me feel too manly
wobbly like this.
I'd just met a real jim dandy.
too soon to think of kiss?
back then yes, too soon to think of kiss!

as we began to walk away
our hands entwined as one
I noticed Helen slightly sway,
weak legs from love is fun.

there was nothing I could do
my hand steadied her around.
Helens knees were goofy too,
at park bench we sat down.

sat on that bench there in the park,
held hands and talked of things.
held hands and talked long after dark
as our hearts learned how to sing.

walked Helen home too late that night,
cause each other we did please.
met dad on porch, beneath porch light,
I was quite ill at ease.

she held my hand, dad this is jim,
jack introduced us in the park.
I like him dad, really like him,
we lost time there in the dark.

her dad and I we talked a while
about most anything.
I'd glance at Helens little smile
and my heart would almost sing.

Helens dad went into bed
before he left to "Helen" said,
guess I'll see more of him.
to me, goodnight jim.

daddy likes you I can tell,
you two will get along.
he knows I really think you're swell,
then softly hummed a song.

this special night was not the last,
I cherished the love that came to pass.

we held hands for a while more
n the lateness of the hour.
tomorrow she must work at store
but her eyes I still devour.

no hugs, no kisses, that's all right.
we held hands and said goodnight.
this was about the tenth of june
still holding hands were we.
two nights later a full clear moon,
tonight a kiss? we'll see.

.as I walked home this lovely miss
we tarried for a while.
beneath the moon, shared our first kiss,
our hearts went kind of wild.

it was great, real good, real grand,
my chest near burst with feeling.
I'm glad, sure glad that I'm a man,
but my heart and head are reeling.

these feelings I'd not had before,
never close in my young life.
I want these feelings more and more,
need Helen for my wife.

while holding Helen close to me
on my chest her head does rest.
my heart does sing, but it's not free,
those feelings were the best!

it's tied and bound by Helens charms,
entwined with Helen in my arms.

for two more weeks both day and night,
a time our hearts did glow.
we walked and talked,
held hands, held tight,
my heart just seemed to grow.

I couldn't know in one more week
as love flowed thru my heart,
a war would end what my soul did seek
and forever we would part.

we talked about our future life
and babies, four or five.
how someday we'd be man and wife
'twas heaven to be alive.

twenty-fifth of june—'twas on that day,
my war that day would start.
the north Koreans stopped our play
tomorrow we must part.

that night as we strolled around
in sarrow we did walk.
in sadness Helens tears flowed down,
too miserably to talk.

we held each other much, much more,
our hearts mixed love with woe.
it's very sad to leave to war,
ten thousand miles away I'll go.

the special feelings we both shared
for the last three weeks or so,
the special way that we both cared,
to leave her, god, please no!

even tho we both did grieve,
there's no way I would stay.
my honor, duty, to war I'll leave
and cherish the love she gave.

just one more night of her warm arms
we held each other tight.
just one more night of Helens charms
we held and held all night.

today I have to catch a bus
a sad time this has been.
.no family there, just two of us,
don't let this be the end.

held each other; can't let go,
the time is running fast.
Helen and I we both do know
we'll say good-bye at last.

the bus will leave before too long
dear god why can't I stay?
I get on board and I'll be gone,
will be the end of play.

I got on board and took my place,
the sadness in me swelled.
outside my window, Helens face.
wish war would rot in hell.

tears and hurt there deep inside,
the last I saw her running beside
the bus, with arms outstretched for me.
her standing in the street alone,
defined our love, our misery.

I rode the bus out to fort ord,
a ship near there I got aboard.
ship took me 'cross the wide wide sea.
my love's ten thousand miles from me.

we sailed to sasebo and then
on to pusan; my war began.
my Helen wrote me every day
love thru her pen would flow.
her longing, loving hopes she'd say.
dear god, I missed her so.

my Helen's arms filled me with joy
and I remembered it so well.
now I'm a lonely boy missing
stuck in mans warring hell.

war is a very lonely place
in this far off killing land.
her letters let me see her face,
in my mind I'd hold her hand.

none knew when our mail call would be
the front kept shifting 'round.
but always letters there for me
from this soul mate I'd found.

sometimes there could be ten or more,
the reading felt divine.
from future wife who I adore,
made me forget my warring time.

my heart was always swelled with love,
I still thank god whose up above,
for those first seven months or more
her letters helped me cope with war.

the last one came in early spring
black was edged around the thing.
"my darling jim's" how it began,
I left it—went to "no mans land".

sat out there t'wixt foe and friend,
wanting hurt; the hurt to end.
hand on gun and head on knee
my buddies came and rescued me.

.I thank them now; I didn't then.
just wanted hurt; the hurt to end.

the hurt did finally go away
but it came back again today.
tho only as I read these rhymes,
they take me back to missing times.

long time ago my Helen died,
I heard of it,I never cried.
for all these years we've been apart,
"my Helen" rests here in my heart.

jimmie joe

more odds n' ends

"My Helens" epilogue

I wrote my poem of Helen
and little did I know.
that as I read it over
all this hurt would show.

sometime before or after that
my eyes turned dull, or dead or flat.
there is no way I can explain
what takes away the conscious pain
and stores it way in back of head.
for future times; or till I'm dead.

subconscious mind can hide away
the sights and pains of warring days.
but as the months or years slide past
the piper will be paid at last.

I assumed the hurt was long, long past,
I'd went to no mans land.
I could have made that day my last,
had pain my heart, my head won't stand.
alone now in this warring land.

hand on gun and head on knee
my buddies came and rescued me.
it's o.k., sarge, come on my friend,
come back with us; it's not the end.

I'd grieved three hours, maybe more,
subconscious mind the pain did store,
back there with other hurts from war.

I stored it well my Helen dear,
thru rhymes I've found it.
it's still here.

I didn't weep, don't need relief
once hurt's hid in back of brain.
it's only now I feel deep grief,
guess now's my time to cope with pain.

sorry there wasn't time back then
forgive me if I cry my friend.

in my poem we're both still young
guess that's the way we'll stay.
in my mind I'm sure we will
that has to be okay.

I'm sorry that you died so young
when I heard I never cried.
it's only that I'd kept the pain
stored somewhere deep inside.

in rhyming my Helen I've let hurt out,
don't think my friends will see.
they would not know what it's about
it's meant for her and me.

the poem reminds my heart of things
I pray you have your angel's wings,
that happened way back then
I'll see you; don't know when
and I'll have you close again.

the time will come I'll have to leave
the ones I love down here.
I'll try, I'll try, to just believe
you're waiting for me, dear.

I'll never know what might have been,
I've wondered every now and then.
what could have been was not to be
come the next life; perhaps we'll see.

I hold three loves within my heart,
june, norma and my Helen.
my Helen takes the largest part
don't know the reason why.
while rhyming certain parts of it
my heart, my soul does cry.

it's been more then forty seven years
since we walked and held back there.
after forty seven years
why would my heart still care?

june and norma softly rest,
all three cause my heart to glow.
.in my heart—still Helen's best.
why this is? I just don't know.

now I am thru, I'll rhyme no more
of long past love that's lost.
no more of pain, of joy, of war.
or "ghosts" I hope I've tossed.

jimmie joe

I wrote alone and really tried
to write my feelings down.
in parts I wrote, in parts I cried,
I had to get it written,
down before I died.

I love you "dad".

odds n' ends

Reality (one of the first poems written)

"Reality" might not be real
it's as close as I can get.
It kind of shows the way I feel.
sadness is part of it.

Sadness for some friends who died
buried I don't know where.
Sadness for the ones who cried
for loss of loved ones there.

Sadness for some friends that lived,
for the cross that they will bear.
I hope somehow they all forgive,
"this land that didn't care".

Anger plays a larger part.
at the time we didn't know,
homeland ignored us from the start.
What's real was TV shows.

There's anger, hurt hid deep inside,
didn't know 'til I wrote these rhymes.
You've spurned us, smothered up the pride,
we should feel from warring times.

That's the way you were; that's fine.
"Forgotten War" the name fits well
that bloody first damn year.
Forgotten too was frozen hell
and Pusan Perimeter.

Five to six million people died
on that small Korean ground.
While most Americans did hide.
They heard no battle sounds,
as canasta made its rounds.

They didn't see the little Children
with a parent not around.
Where the hell's the parent?
Damn you they're in the ground,
while starving children wander 'round.

They didn't see the massacred civilians
or P.O.W.s murdered there.
They didn't see the dying children.
I have to wonder, would they care?

There was not the coverage
we later had on TV screen.
Maybe it would have been different
if they'd shared the sights we'd seen.

I know they'd take defensive mode
and say how wrong I am.
Our coming home they didn't care.
neither Korea nor Vietnam.

If you didn't care about your sons
who you sent off to war,
Why would you care for other ones,
who suffer death on distant shore?

Again tell me how you cared.
Please tell me just once more!

No parades and not one cheer
as we left at start of war.
The first of us fought for a year.
We came home; same as before.
No parade and not one cheer.
No welcome home; no, have a beer.

The attitude they all did take?
What's on TV?; my car is new.
have a new boat, it's on the lake.
Helen's gone? To bad for you.

Those things happen, don't you know,
you were gone over a year or so.

Times here have been really good,
the factories are just humming.
This friend he never understood
how my mind he was a bumming.

Thru my rhymes anger will show,
love, sadness and compassion too.
The politicians I've placed below
what pig farmers get on shoes.

Politicians and Mac Arthur
who could not think tactics thru,
have their ticker tape parades,
Dog face? No, no hell no, not you!

Get back in the hole you did not win,
a tie's the best that you could do.
Mac Arthur sucked the Chinese in?
come on, hell, that can't be true!

History will get it recorded right
bout Mac Arthur's tactics there.
history will recorded it right
and damn it no one cares.

It's nothing that our hands were tied
by our politicians here.
There will be no parade for us,
no waving Flag; no cheer.

I can't believe how people were
in those times so long ago.
Can't believe they didn't care
about young men dying over there.

It seems a waste of Warriors lives,
a tragic sacrifice gone awry.
A lot of crying Moms and Wives.
I wonder; why did the Warriors die?

.The civilians by the "millions"
die in warring lands; what for?
in "Vietnam" and "North Korea"
what did us humans gain from war?
A lot of people dying—nothing more!

Politicians I no longer trust
when we go off to war.
We need a cause, a cause that's just,
politicians ask what for?

Americans didn't seem to care
about her fighting men.
They'd had their fill in World War II?
To this I say — Amen!

A bullet killed us just as dead,
hot jagged flying shrapnel too.
We still held dying Buddies,
as you did in world war two.
"Reality's" what we went thru; like you.

July and August have been months' of hell,
I hope September won't be worse.
Artillery, tank and mortar rounds
keep falling like God's curse.

hot jagged shrapnel rips away
some arms, legs, heads or guts.
it's more than some men's minds can take,
today one went quite nuts.

Panic thrashing, legs, arms and knees,
his "screaming soul" could take no more.
Just trying to hide 'neath fallen leaves,
he'd left this godless place of war.
Was the only one I've seen this bad,
it's worse then death; it's worse than sad.

Was an awful scene for men to see,
could it be curse or grace of God?
Well why not you? or why not me?
Sad abhorrent memory.

Next to hell, which is a dread,
that scene caused my greatest fear.
I don't want my mind to leave my head
and lose all thoughts that I hold dear.

Flat dull eyes can cope with death,
can cope with other sights and pain.
I think we never cope with this,
when Buddies mind escapes his brain.

As Commie artillery pounded down
in fox holes we would stay.
Concussion slams us all around,
direct hit would end our day.

When the pounding finally stops
and the flying shrapnel ends,
we can expect our Commie friends.

Do not dig fox holes under trees
the only thing that's worse,
Is for them to use proximity fuse
and fire damn air burst.

From twenty feet or so above
hot shrapnel slices down.
A little gift with Commies love
sends men to "Sacred Ground".

Morphine helped a bit I guess,
near dawn "Fetch" took eternal rest.
A good man died; plus many more.
Many thousands in first year.

American people are tired of war?
They should have raised a bigger fuss.
Wonder what we're fighting for?
Our buddies next to us.

War gave them jobs to buy their toys,
to hell with us their fighting boys.
They bitch at home, enjoy their beer,
while we're still dying over here.

But I digress, these last few rhymes
are not the way I felt back then.
I kind of felt in warring times,
Honor, Duty was to defend
this country that sent me to war,
protect Flag, Country, Home and Friends.

Once in combat mind went blank
about what politicians spiel.
Protecting buddies, destroy a tank,
damn war is all that's real.
"K" rations our next meal

North Korea had many tanks,
South Korea not a one,
Russian made t-34s
with big high velocity guns.

a 3.5 bazooka, a shaped charge in rocket head,
hit the tank just right, bye, bye tank it's dead.

Our tanks arrived they helped a lot
our out gunned infantry.
They worked us out of many spots
and once they rescued me.
Our rations now are "C"

In defensive mode our only job
is to keep the ground we hold.
Commie artillery rounds do lob
for few hours blood runs cold.

This sure is not a pleasant place,
will I live to see my Helens' face?

Thank god we're not on open ground,
as shrapnel rips its holes in air.
Pressed deep in fox hole I am found,
don't like it here; hate it out there.

Then bugles, whistles in the night,
mortars start crashing down.
Machine gun duels and fire fights,
grenades spew shrapnel around.

Commies with fixed bayonets appear
from smoky flare lit gloom.
Guerrillas might attack from rear,
combined could seal our doom.

A lot of times it turns out right.
A few times 'twas a "bloody night".

Guerrilla burp guns in the night,
fire thousand rounds a minute.
Confusing mixed up fire fight
and more good men die in it.

For many men the taps will play.
(They really don't play them here)
Top brass tactics day after day
seem callous and unclear.

The first few months this was the way
under general walkers command.
No offense, defense held sway.
guerrillas ambush in lowlands.

After "Inchon" we broke out,
gave "North Korea" quite a fuss.
We did what infantry's about
top brass no more confined us.

The reason now we got right to it?
more ordinance is supplied.
There's finally enough men to do it,
at last we've turned the tide

Pusan Perimeter was quite a chore,
slowing, then stopping commie reds.
Was time to even up the score
and make them pay for all our dead.

We pushed them north,
we pushed them hard,
near to the Chinese border.
We thought we did a real fine job,
We fulfilled Mac Arthur's order.

I've heard them claim we didn't win
and were not quite up to snuff.
We whipped the North Korean men.
in five months and it was tough.

We pushed them to the "Yalu river"
by nineteen-fifty in November.
Mac Arthur ordered we delivered,
none cared and none remember.

jimmie joe

A hoard of red Chinese did cross
the frozen "Yalu rivers" ice.
For a while I guess they were the boss,
didn't make us feel too nice.

Our supply lines were way too long.
Mac Arthur over extended,
ammo, gas and all supplies
were very soon expended.
Many young lives then ended.

We had no recourse; must retreat,
damn politicians blunder.
Mac Arthur's ego caused defeat,
our victory went asunder.

Truman had ordered Mac Arthur
stay back from Chinese border.
Mac Arthur's stupid ego, disobeyed that order.

The longest retreat America has made
occurred in that frozen land.
Both sides lost a lot of lives.
Politicians accept Mac Arthur's stand.
In World War Two our hero man
there in the wide pacific.
Was then to me, "never again",
the egotist's horrific.

Frozen limbs and frozen feet,
frozen blood sealed up the wounds.
Those who lived thru that cold retreat,
should not forgive, forget real soon.

Frozen bodies there in death,
arms and legs protruding.
It was sad and quite grotesques,
a lot like hell's intruding.

Piled in trucks like cord wood
to some might seem obscene.
They brought out all the bodies.
I salute U.S. Marines.

We didn't whip the Red Chinese.
We push them back to north.
We didn't do it all alone,
the whole U.N. sallied forth.

Politicians say we can't wage war
north of the "Yalu river",
as China's population soars
this war could last forever.

China could funnel men across
the North Korean border.
losing a million men a year,
to Chinese not out of order.

China could lose ten million men
and not feel it too much.
Would we lose a million men to win?
(if yes); you're out of touch.

Few Americans support this war,
we didn't know it then.
It's not the dying they abhor,
it's because we didn't win.

Politics got us in this war.
We didn't lose!!
Politics got us out of this war.
Go walk in politicians shoes.

You dishonor us who fight for you
when total victory's all you crave.
You dishonor us the living.
You dishonor us in graves.

To those who say we didn't win,
every Harry, Dick or Tom.
Did you suggest invade china?
Maybe use the ATOM BOMB?

Your idea of war is from John Wayne,
"You" his manly movies please.
They don't capture real death or pain
or real legs blown off at knees.

You'll never see the flat dull eyes.
(can't be captured on the screen)
from many times of viewing death
or other sights we've seen.

All you bastards oh so brave,
stay home so bored, no strife.
Stay home so safe, yet rant and rave,
while others lose their life.

give another twist to knife.
I got home, we were ignored
like back from a vacation.
It's been a year? we're glad you're here
lets watch new TV station.

We're really glad you're home you know.
It's time for "Ed Sullivans" TV show.
Welcome home my friend

That was the attitude back then
in August of fifty-one.
They ignored this little nowhere war.

World War Two had just been won.

I had to fudge the last few rhymes,
did not know what to do.
I have no memory of being home,
till early nineteen fifty two.

I remember getting on the plane
to Chicago we did fly.
High above the Rockies,
my memory said bye, bye.
I have no idea why.

I can't recall how I got home
or seeing family or my friends.
I can't recall most anything
'til after my furlough ends.

My mind's still blank
thru those times at home.
I've tried hard to recall.
I can't; can't remember much at all.

I can recall being back at base
and the platoon that I did train.
Subconscious mind would not release
this war that fogged my brain.

I trained men then and some would die,
for two more years the war would last.
I never, never ask me why,
the dying time is long time past.

Spent time in hospital down there,
the world had turned to not quite real.
I'd developed tunnel vision
was a scary way to feel.

257

Sights and sounds were far away.
Quite confused in bed I'd lay.

It lasted just a week or two
and I was back to training men.
Took all subconscious mind could do
to keep the ghosts locked in.

I know how odd to some this seems,
even my subconscious was locked tight.
Took two more years to start war dreams
and fight alone in dark of night.

I married on December twenty nine
of nineteen fifty one.
My memory started to return,
(thru sex? because it's fun?)
From here on out my memory's?
Almost o.k., (as it should be).

Discharged June 10th. of fifty two,
went to civilian life.
Civilians attitude about the war
caused my brain a bit of strife.

No one cared; didn't give a damn
about our fighting men.
This attitude it really stayed,
even after war did end.

Everyone I knew felt that way,
my family, wife and friends.
Americans I'm sad to say
betrayed their warrior men.

I have many thoughts within my head,
been flitting out thru time,
about all the humans wars make dead,
the damn killing warring slime.

Politicians have complete control
of most armies all world wide.
They're the ones who I do hold
responsible for all who died.

For P.O.W.s left to their fate,
abandoned by Congress in their halls.
Some politicians I must hate,
a group of slime with traitors balls.

I feel my homeland does not care
about our warriors so long dead.
All these rhymes I hope reveal,
each life lost in war is real.

We have a tendency to think
of young men we send to war.
As masses without faces,
please think of them as more.

They're average age is twenty
life song has just begun,
their dreams were all the same as ours,
they're not some faceless ones.

Think of them as your Brother,
Grandpa, Uncle or your Dad.
They died for us in battle
not to remember is quite sad.

Think of sweethearts, Wives or Mothers
when word came back their Warrior died,
think of all the deep, deep sadness
years and tears will never hide.
After while—Just hide inside.

Somehow I want us all to feel
as Moms do about a Son.
That warriors death is very real,
he is not a faceless one.

If fifty thousand die in war
those numbers don't mean much.
Like child's tin soldiers nothing more,
they look the same and dress the same,
but each had a life, each had a name.

They're not tin soldiers, not the same,
for us each one does die.
As a thousand spirits drift to sky,
just one tin soldier rides away?

War is not a song we play.
If it is a song the tune's to death
and pain and misery.

The grim reaper will decides who's left
to write the war songs history.

If fifty thousand Mothers cry
us their pain will touch.
Moms aren't ten thousand miles away,
they live quite close to us.
They remember,
Walking David to the bus.

In world war two a Star of Gold
in home of dead Warriors Mom was placed.
Korea and Vietnam,
did someone show the place?

The Marble Wall with all those names
inscribed in marble black,
brings back reality with pain
each young warrior won't be back.

He died for more than you or me
in that far off killing land.
He died to make the oppressed free?
God let that be true,
please help us know and understand.

Any Warriors name on Marble Wall
will be sadly praised by me.
Inscribed in marble they will stay
and all who visit there will know,
he lived.

The ground around this Honour Wall
on which the caring trod,
absorbs the tears of one and all
as prayers are sent to god.

At Unknown Soldiers grave we grieve.
Black Marble wall? Death we believe.

Medals, flowers and tears all lay
at base of wall where caring pray.
All my rhymes I wrote for you,
"Korea", World Wars One and Two.
mostly for "Korea" and "Vietnam".
to show them some still give a damn.

Korean Memorial brings no pain,
somehow it doesn't make me feel.
Squad formation walks in rain,
a Warriors name is all that's real.

Each statue stands, each has a gun,
without the names they're faceless ones.
Fifty-four thousand of our sons.

Without a name to read and touch,
the image we still hold in,
a Soldiers Statue still portrays,
one Tin Soldier made of Tin.

"The Vietnam Memorial".

The names show that death was real.
The warriors spirits us surround.
The warriors spirits make us feel
the power of this sacred ground.

Not for the death of thousands.
It's to the death of a Mothers Son.
It's to the death of one young Warrior
whose life had just begun.

It's only to the death of one.
Husband? - Father? - Brother? - Son?

The Wall

The Vietnam Memorial is nearly sacred in my mind, it causes sadness to well up in my heart that is far and above any other memorial, book, movie or any thing I can name in this world. The Vietnam Black Wall of Honour seems to hold an aurora of Spirits that are to me tangible. Those Spirits are there for us, they heal us, be we Vietnam Vets, Korean Vets or any combat Vets.

It is a Wondrously unique and therapeutic oasis for the hidden recesses of a pained soul. A soul who has lived the reality of a war zone and survived, survived to discover a war doesn't end just because he came home. Some need an oasis such as the **"Black Marble Wall"**.

The healing is a sadness, sadness is a part of healing and it's okay to cry my Warrior Brothers. Tears are part of sadness. Tears are part of healing.

jimmie joe
fishhook junction, alaska

a family in a killing zone

civilians have the worse in war
untold millions of them die.
massacred by the enemy or
bombs falling from the sky.

killed by hunger and disease,
the mothers weep in pure despair.
think of this I ask you please,
the little children dying there.

think of the lands we fight wars in
as your town or state back here.
think of your family and your friends
for their safety how you'd fear.
terror for all that you hold dear.

think of massacred civilians
as you flee to get away.
think of how there is no safety,
it goes on day after day.
nothing helps, but still you pray.

moms won't have a husband there
all have been conscripted.
children's safety's in your care.
some mothers will not make it when,
raped and killed by devil men.

so we have our little children,
alone wandering thru your land.
some with missing arms or legs,
none to give a helping hand.
their purgatory caused by man.

think of bombers overhead
dropping bombs day after day,
maiming killing those around you.
hide in fear and pray and pray.
god stop this war, please god today.

why doesn't god stop warring land,
is heaven or hell his only end?
god's tough for me to understand,
chaplains didn't help my friend.

desperate search for food and shelter
as slowly children die.
every thing is helter-skelter
again bombs falling from the sky.

think of holding injured children,
won't be any doctor there.
how to keep your child from dying
there's no help not anywhere.
does your god hear a child in prayer?

guardian angles have to cry?
I think the guardians said good-bye.
all these rhymes are meant to tell,
that "all involved in war face hell".

this is no exaggeration.
I need me to understand.
why do we accept? how do we stop
all this killing done by man?

five billion prayers for peace we send,
still wars go on, wars do not end.

our wars have been across the seas
young men go there to fight.

Americans have never known
the sound of bombers in the night.

never known the hopelessness and fear
of death that comes in many ways.
wars happen over there not here,
here our safe families grow and play.
sunday church? have a nice day.

most don't have a problem
with genocide in far off lands.
as long as all our children
are safe from wars' grim reapers hands.

food for children's' bellies please,
doctors, hospitals and schools.
our wars are fought across the seas
we who don't care are selfish fools.
I hope that we would care much more,
if we really knew the pains of war.

these millions of dead civilians
are too much to comprehend.
below are examples of our major wars,
counting all the bush wars many more.

over one hundred million dead
in world wars one and two.
"Korea" lost several million more,
several million in "Vietnam" died from war.

in bush wars millions more were killed.
it kind of seems like mankind
in killing the innocent is skilled.
all civilians all long dead,
why? I can not understand.

I'm almost ashamed to be a man.
too much death, pain and misery.
is genocide ———— humanity?
is it a part of you and me?

millions have died from bombs or gun.
as you read don't think of them.
I ask you please— "just think of one".

your child, or little baby,
your mother, or your dad,
your brother, or your sister,
grandmother, or granddad?

so many ways there are to die
in lands where wars are fought.
not just bombs falling from the sky,
the refugees are all distraught
by raping, killing devil men.

disease and hunger kill young and old,
girls and women are soldiers toys.
many die from freezing cold.

without shelter they can't survive.
some just don't want to stay alive.
at times it's right — their "suicide".

these happened in those killing lands,
in every tragic place of war.
I need for me to understand
all this and much, much more.
guess that's what I'm writing for.

I don't know how we will atone.
about two hundred million dead civilians,
in this century alone.

they just estimate the numbers.
they can not do any more.
along with all those people,
most all records destroyed by war.
wonder why? certain politicians I abhor.

I had to show a part of me
the ones I love don't know.
there might be some don't like it
but that "is" the way it goes.

the rhymes that follow page after page,
reflect my thoughts, "my pain, my rage".

it's time I show some (children grown)
who blamed young men for "vietnam",
that all the warring seeds were sown?
they'll know "if" they read my poem.
to some it will not mean a wit,
some family and some friends, toss it away
don't read it, if you my poem offends.

I'm hoping as I write these rhymes,
there will be some that understand?
you don't have to be a warrior,
to question the why of killing lands.

why Mac Arthur pushed to Chinas border
causing thousands more to die.
why he disobeyed president Truman's' order
and congress did not reply.

why our politicians didn't try
to find a peaceful way.
why we had the gulf of Tonkin lie,
why our congress said okay.

why millions of innocent civilians lay
dead long before their natural time.
why the worlds damn politicians play
uncaring and safe from warring slime.

why some expanded wars took place
for generals ego alone.
why some took place to save the face
of presidents safe at home.

The killing zones in Vietnam

Free fire Zones

The Hague and Geneva convention laws?

Free fire zones are generally huge areas where anything that moves can be fired on. In my mind it was a policy approaching war crimes, conceived by the frustrated Generals and sanctioned by our politicians of that time. add body counts as a method of determining how a war is going and the end result is apt to be a "My Lai".

As we lose tract of the sacredness of innocent Human life we are very much in danger of losing what keeps us free. the policy of free fire zones and body counts was no excuse for the massacre. The blame is not just those officers and men in the field, it is equally shared up the chain of command, thru the joint chief's of staff to the president. Congress had a duty of oversight of our military and the Commander-in-Chiefs' policies, not battle tactics but the policies that disregard the sanctity of innocent lives.

I honor the warriors who fought in Vietnam, My Lai was an *anomaly* and was terribly wrong, the fact that in twelve years of guerrilla war there weren't more My Lai's is a tribute to our men. The fact that America erupted in disbelief and anger when the cover-up was revealed is a huge plus for Americas' perception of what we should be, it was the beginning of the end of an unjust policy out of control.

Give us well trained Officers and Noncoms who have honor and discipline, we'll give you back no more My Lai's.

Give us honorable politicians who insist we adhere to the laws of land warfare and we'll give you armed forces that would not commit a My Lai. Give us presidents who have the balls to prosecute those who commit war crimes. Friend or foe, atrocities are a capital crime. Calley escaped nearly scot-free, his men? Nothing.

Equally give us a "just cause" next time you ask us to fight a war for you, not one that is so questionable it divides a nation.

I guess it's time for me to quit,
I don't think I'm wrong in what I say.
For me I've said bout all of it and
God bless the USA.

jimmie joe,
fishhook junction, alaska

****

There is a bit of guilt I feel
over things I'd no control.
facts I didn't know back then,
know them now, the facts are old.

guilt for the devastation
wreaked on north Korean towns.
was the policy of my nation
to flatten most all down.

a lot of the towns that I went thru
north of the thirty-eighth parallel,
didn't seem to be military targets,
still bombers blew most all to hell.

the war then was only four months old,
thirty two more months the bombers flew.
a few million civilians died.
they must hate those bomber crews.

we dropped bombs nearly every day
from twenty thousand feet or more.
I guess that we can safely say
we didn't aim at them; that's war.

when a few million civilians die
because there's no place to hide,
can't escape the terror from the sky,
is honor, really honor on our side?

laws of land warfare were made
to protect defenseless ones.
laws of land warfare were made
after the end of world war one.

the hague and geneva convention laws
to bombers don't apply, that's true,
please will someone tell me why?

we had to study land warfare laws
back in nineteen forty nine.
living by that "honour"
"kept me a friend of mine"

from several thousand feet or more,
they don't see civilians die
or kids with missing limbs from war.
they can't see the mothers cry,
holding babies as they die.
it's just collateral damage?
collateral damage from the sky.

germany and japan bombed civilians
many times in world war two.
we used those same damn tactics,
we bombed civilians too.

wasted japan and europe's towns,
blew damn near every building down.
it became accepted way of war
till exposed on world TV.
dead civilians we abhor
(if they're white like you and me.)

I think we told honor good-bye
with all the innocent we killed
from dumb bombs falling from the sky.
it's tough for me to justify.

I sure hope I am not alone
in feeling that I should atone.
for acts I didn't do.

we got it right in ninety-one,
with smart bombs in that war.
civilians killed were very few,
not in the millions like before.

in future wars we'll probably fight,
lets keep civilian dead real lite.

now commie cadre I can hate,
they commit murder on the ground.
they kill the defenseless face to face,
they use clubs or gun them down.

bayonets and fire too,
they bury some alive,
I've seen results of all these deeds
where defenseless won't survive

these men who think they have no soul
I hope that they will see,
there is a God; they go to hell.
but not for eternity.

some old men have been in battle,
question what is right or wrong.
question politicians prattle as they
quest their warring song.

some old men realize that war
is something all should now deplore.
some old men are like a bully
beating kids outside the schools.
some old men are just damn fools
when they call for devastation,
the hell with civilian population.

some old men, we're safe back here,
relive "glories"? of the past.
vote to send young men to war,
how long will this crap last?

I repeat a truth

Damn the worlds politicians, the safe, fat, contemptuous, flag waving bastards who consider a crime against Humanity as something only the loser can commit and/or be prosecuted for. The egotistical asses never even consider that "war itself is a crime against Humanity"

On the other side of this coin is a statement that is equally true, but the cases are rarer than the world seems to believe. "A crime against Humanity" is the abstention from intervening and preventing crimes against Humanity by the power of governments against their own peoples.

we glorify the civil war and
world war one and two.
those were necessary wars,
we did what we had to do.

I question the "Korean war",
the one we don't remember.
I knew what we were fighting for
till nineteen fifty, late november.

state department could have kept
china from coming in.
congress also was inept
malfeasance was their sin.
will it happened once again?

back then it was the old men,
politicians who we trusted,
they let us down they didn't care
too late Mac Arthur, Truman busted.

again I am thru, I'll rhyme no more
of long past love that's lost.
no more of pain, of joy, of war.
or "ghosts" I hope I've tossed.

jimmie joe

About the author, James Joseph Woods,

RA16 307 188 — MOS 1745

jimmy joe — "Boy", the author when he was young, a naive farm boy, a skipper of schooling for fishing. Born October 11, 1930.

"Old Gent" — A dog Boy loved throughout his childhood, a wondrous dog, a healing dog. I miss "Old Gent".

jimmy joe — My first love Helen's nickname when she was a little tike, I have no idea why, she was a woman (long deceased), who completely stole my heart.

jimmy joe — My little Son who died in Nineteen fifty-four, a Dandy, happy Boy. I miss the little Fella throughout my years.

Eisenhower's papers, regarding his knowledge of the POWs left in North Korea, which I read in1997, were the stimuli I needed to start this book. I was so full of disbelief, rage and disappointment with my country I had to have an outlet. Disbelief is gone, the rage and disappointment will probably remain until my ashes are scattered on a peaceful Alaskan cove. Long before I finished my writings rage had subsided; there is only a deep anger when I think of those Boys lives after their betrayal. I still can't believe our government could do such .... They can and they did. It is now difficult for me think of my Country as Honourable, in every war they have knowingly left our men in the enemies hellish grasp.

I began writing for my own need, I now write for Comrades of long ago and to expose our young people to the pains of war rather than to the Glory of the battle or stories of the killing.

For many the last ground battle does not end a war, especially wars that do not measure up to the standard of acceptance by America's public, the ones that are not quite "real wars". Wars that have no parades before, during or after are wars without a tangible cause, the public is not aroused, and the war is not justified. There is no real enemy for the American people to rally against.

I lost my Wife in 1966 and for the next sixteen years I raised Children. My times of real contentment have been when my Children and Grandchildren were small, holding them as I sang, walking with them while they held my finger. Showing them the wonders of nature, hearing all their "whys" and not being able to answer most as it seemed to just bring another "why". Now I have Great Grandchildren for sharing these treasured times.

Catch those fish in places wild? My lord blessed me; Alaska has been a great place to live. I am thankful I moved here forty years ago. I love this land. I love her Oceans, Mountains, Wildness and the Peace I have found while fishing her waters. I've seen the Northern Lights rippling across the entire sky in displays of shimmering colors only God could mix, leaving me in awe I still recall, awe I still feel. Alaska, my Alaska is a wondrous land, a healing land.

Most subjects I cover in my poems by necessity are unpleasant, not what my life's been about. The years1950/51 spent as a Combat Infantryman in Korea were only a background, a place just beyond my conscious mind, a reality I kept hidden. They became desperation in the foreground one night in 1989; my Angel must have saved me from my own hand. It would take nine more years and this book for my final healing. I do not know why it took nearly fifty years to come full circle. I fought my way thru alone, I wrote alone and except for one time, I cried alone

Boys journey's was long, he was given no map, no compass and no direction for years. I took Boys hand and we unwrapped time thru these pages, while unlocking Boys tomb of pain I wept. As I shed tears Boy had stored for nearly fifty years my journey took me thru his distant maze of time and sorrow. At some point I found I could not release Boys Hand, I was trapped into finishing I knew not what. I couldn't stop until "Little Children—Grown-ups War" appeared in the last room of a young Soldiers tomb of pain. Opening it was tough, really tough. My journey from the mists of fifty years begins, *take my hand my Son, we're going Home.*

jmmie joe,
fishhook junction, alaska

Printed in the United States
4131